GOOD FOR YOUR BABY— EASY FOR YOU!

Find out how quick, simple, and economical it can be to make your own baby food—with recipes for . . .

- CHICKEN PUREE
- MUSHROOM MARVEL SOUP
- STUFFED POTATOES
- GREEN BEANS AND APRICOTS
- PASTA PLEASERS
- SWEET POTATO FINGER FOODS
  AND MORE!

BABY EATS!

Baby Eats!

LOIS SMITH

BERKLEY BOOKS, NEW YORK

BABY EATS!

A Berkley Book / published by arrangement with
the author

PRINTING HISTORY
Berkley edition / June 1994

ISBN: 0-425-14120-9

BERKLEY®
Berkley Books are published by The Berkley Publishing Group,
200 Madison Avenue, New York, New York 10016.
The name BERKLEY and the "B" design
are trademarks belonging to the Berkley Publishing Corporation.

PRINTED IN THE UNITED STATES OF AMERICA

10 9 8 7 6

Dedication

I dedicate this book to my three daughters, Julie, Collette, and Allison—the loves of my life. Over the years, it is likely that I have produced about 25,000 meals in which one or more of my beauties has shared communication, bonding, and wonderful foods. The time has finally come when there are no more birds in the nest to nurture; no more excursions to provide the daily nourishment. It is time to share the memories and the things that have been learned.

Acknowledgments

Among my reference papers are some articles on natural foods from the 1930s. My mother, a natural foods advocate, read, experimented, and studied diligently. Her early research resulted in my own very strong body, mind, and interest in carrying on the family tradition of good, fresh, nutritious foods. Her name was Rachel Millikin and she lived eighty-seven good years.

Paul S. Berry, M.D., is a young doctor who has the sensitivity and dedication of old time doctors—doctors who took the time to talk with their patients and listen. Paul told me I could do this work and he was right. Without his support, this book would not be.

Pansy Kaperonis-Dzilvelis is the mother of four children, the last of whom is graduating from college. Pansy almost owned the chair next to mine at the computer. Her gently offered suggestions and love for children and foods greatly enhanced this book. Whenever the project was losing momentum, she offered creative suggestions and allowed me to visit with the babies and toddlers at her child care facility. I could see for myself how flowers, animals, trees, and gentle breezes enhance baby meals.

Karen Strohecker writes her own cookbooks but unselfishly contributed her support to this book. I could always count on Karen for the enticing aromas wafting through her home, exquisite food beautifully served, and thoughtful contributions to the book from her extensive culinary experience. She sustained the author.

Harold Goldstein, Director of Healthy Los Angeles 2000, under the direction of the County of Los Angeles Department of Health Services, is dedicated to promoting health and preventing disease. As this book goes to press, he is supporting our efforts to bring nutritional information to pregnant mothers throughout the county. His interest has been a great sustainer in our efforts to help mothers give the best to their babies and toddlers.

My special thanks go to Pauline Krips, my attorney friend, who dispenses reason and clarity as no one else I know. The fish sections of the book are largely the result of Pauline's special love of seafood and the many ways she has experimented with those tender gifts from the sea.

There is no special significance to the order in which these acknowledgments of deep caring and concern appear. With that, the next in line is Jo Anne De Voe, who loads her car with toys and special gifts for underserved children on a regular basis. Her technical support has been invaluable and her contribution great. Jo Anne has nourished her children and grandchildren and is certain that good food can make this world better.

My brother, Ken Millikin, and I grew up having ground fig and nut candy in our Christmas stockings, whole grain breads, fresh fruits, and vegetables from our own land. Ken won a chemistry scholarship many moons ago and has been involved in using his knowledge of chemistry to balance nature ever since. His input has been only a phone call away and his patience without limit in helping with this work.

Johanna Asarian-Anderson, Nutrition Program Coordinator for Los Angeles County, has given me insight into government-supplied information as it relates to pregnant women and babies. Her personal interest in and contribution to improving health and nutrition for babies is outstanding.

Toni Lopopolo, my agent, is filled with joy and enthusiasm. Her spirits carried this book to its happy conclusion.

My editor, Heather Jackson, displayed unyielding patience and willingly shared her wisdom, encouraging this author's best efforts.

It has been our good fortune to have frequent contact with those acknowledged in these pages. Unfortunately, one of those very dedicated people could not be reached before this printing. My twins' pediatrician passed away, which was a tremendous loss both to the twins, my other daughter, Julie, and me. His memory lives on in this book, through his encouragement on our home-produced baby foods, and his careful analysis of the results.

Trenton, Madison, and Laura can't read or talk yet but I still want to thank them for letting me feed them, smiling at the flavors, and being just who they are—wonderful babies.

Contents

Contents

Baby Eats!

Introduction

In my maternity business I talked with hundreds of pregnant women. Some were in the first trimester of pregnancy, while others appeared to be a breath away from labor. As we offered information about subjects such as delivery rooms, breast feeding, and baby care, it became increasingly apparent that most pregnant women had not learned enough information about baby care to feel comfortable and safe.

In the three hours that we conducted our educational meetings, we did not explore the subject of homemade baby foods. Not one future mother ever asked about infant nutrition. That is not to say that there could not have been an interest in the subject. The lack of curiosity was more the result of too much important information being given in a short period of time.

Clearly, what a baby eats will affect his entire life. If a child is suffering from allergies, he may not be aware of the discomfort that he feels in a way that he can express. At school he may become irritable, inattentive or show other behaviors that impede his maximum learning ability.

Allergies aside, proper nutrition will not only help babies build strong bodies but will help their bodies' immune systems fight infection. Every parent wants the very best for

1

their children, so the real question must be, how does one provide the best foods?

Food safety is part of the answer to good nutrition. We have always looked to government agencies to regulate safety and trusted that what is available to us in stores is not hazardous. Recent studies warn of "a potential concern that some children may be ingesting dangerous amounts of pesticides."* We hope that this book will offer some positive direction toward safeguarding you and your children from this potential problem.

Opinions of experts vary, but all agree that, although many fruits and vegetables are subjected to pesticides, we need fruits and vegetables in our diets. When parents buy fresh produce, they have more control than when buying canned or frozen foods (unless they are labeled as containing only organically grown ingredients). Fresh organic produce is available in most major chain stores and many independent stores. Organic foods are usually identified as such by label.

I like to explain the benefits of good food in a rather simplistic way. Each baby is born with a set of conditions based on genes, birth, and other factors. Some infants are born stronger and some weaker with strengths and weaknesses in different areas of the body. I like to think of it as the difference between a very powerful car and a weak car—each with different carburetors. In either case, regular maintenance and good, pure fuel will provide the best performance. Each car has its own "best" fuel. And so it is with humans. Each body has its own food needs to grow and function best. Good maintenance is providing a nurturing environment, proper rest, and an endless amount of love.

*L.A. Times, June 29, 1993.

How important will food be in your little person's life? Very important. It's at the top of the priority list. From ancient times, when feasts worshipping Bacchus were called "bacchants," to the present, with power lunches at the Polo Lounge, food sets the mood. Breaking bread together has always been used to form bonds between people. There can be no more rewarding bond than the bond between parent and child, so please make meal times wonderful!

Preparation

GETTING READY

Equipment options for preparing homemade baby foods are listed on the following pages. Many of the items are probably in your kitchen now and most of the things that you need will be useful even after your baby has ceased to eat baby foods.

You can prepare most of the food items in this book with a very few pieces of cookware/apparatus. Perhaps it is more convenient to have a wide selection of equipment, but it is not necessary. Try to purchase only those items that will provide long-term usefulness in your cookery.

Many times in this book, we will remind you that your intimate knowledge of your baby's needs, growth, and reactions must be communicated by you to your pediatrician. He can then give you his best advice about when to start the baby on more solid foods, what to feed him, and what dietary changes are needed as the baby develops.

Each baby's food plan will be distinctly his. Every baby is different in many ways; family allergy patterns, development, and personal tastes differ.

There are many food lists in this book. The first list is intentionally short and deals with first foods. Your doctor must review those specific foods to make his recommendation for your baby's food plan. Later in the book, you will find more complete lists of foods, herbs, and spices for your doctor's approval or disapproval. Do follow his advice carefully and work together as a team.

Trying every recipe in the book will not produce a better baby. We created a variety of foods to give you ideas and choices. Now it is up to the baby to let you know what he likes and what he dislikes.

The steps are easy:

- COOK
- PUREE
- FEED BABY
- FREEZE EXCESS FOOD
- WARM
- AND DO IT ALL OVER AGAIN!

EQUIPMENT FOR FOOD PREPARATION

It is helpful to become familiar with equipment options before you choose what best fits your family. The list of equipment in this section is not intended as a purchasing guide.

Equipment for pureeing, blending, grinding, and chopping

Hand turned food mill
Electric minichopper/grinder
Hand-held, wand-style blender
Regular blender
Food processor

Tools for straining and steam cooking
Tea sieve with handle or chain
Several sizes of food strainers (including ¼ cup size)
Cone-shaped colander with wooden presser
Collapsible steamer basket
Asparagus pan with wire basket insert

Various pans and skillets of your choice
Normal cookware to suit your basic cooking needs will
suffice for making baby food.

Cutting surfaces
Wooden cutting board
Plastic cutting board

Other kitchen tools
Knives: paring, chopping, and carving
Metal and rubber spatulas
Grater
Wood spoons
Measuring spoons
Measuring cups
Mixing bowls
Ice cube trays
4-ounce containers with lids (moisture and vapor proof)
Sets of storage trays and food containers
Plastic wrap
Tape

INFORMATION ABOUT EQUIPMENT

Regular blenders

A blender is probably the most important purchase for making your baby foods. Almost any foods that you will serve your small baby can be processed in a blender.

It is very important to select a blender with a strong motor. Considering the types of materials that you will be pureeing and the frequency of use, a weak motor may burn out. It is truly cost-effective to buy a good blender.

A helpful hint for pureeing meat: Cube in ½-inch pieces and add fluids. Preparing small quantities of meat is the best way to protect the motor. Vegetables and fruits can be processed in larger quantities with no damage done.

Minichopper/grinder

A two-speed minichopper/grinder is very handy for producing small batches of food for one meal. This item can puree a variety of foods. Cereals, such as oatmeal, can be ground to a very fine texture and bananas can be processed—two beginning foods no mother can do without.

Hand-held, wand-style blender

This is a hand-held blender which can be placed into the food container. It is quick to clean. Placing the knife end into a glass of water and turning the blender on will dislodge any food and quickly clean the appliance. The wand is handy for preparing malts, yogurts, and other soft foods.

Food mill

Food mills come in several sizes and are hand operated. They are particularly handy for parents who wish to prepare foods for the baby when they are away from home. In a restaurant it is often possible to prepare a baby's meal using a food mill; vegetables and some softer meats that are served in restaurants will grind nicely in one. Most food mills are easy to transport and easy to clean. They are also handy at home for small projects.

Steam baskets and asparagus pan

Collapsible steam baskets are the most common item for keeping foods out of water and allowing them to be cooked by steam. They come in various sizes. The size of your pan dictates what size steam basket you will use.

The asparagus pan is tall and slender and has a wire basket inside. This is useful in preparing a multitude of foods, as they can be layered. Foods requiring longer cooking will be placed on the bottom, additional foods can be added at a later time. When steaming several different types of vegetables, you can shake the steam basket gently, releasing the vegetables onto a platter, and keeping each vegetable type separate. This has many applications and is especially convenient when you are preparing different steamed foods for adults and the baby.

Storage containers

It is convenient to have containers that hold small amounts of food and are vapor proof and moisture proof. When ice trays are used, plastic wrap and tape will cover and seal the food sufficiently.

Purchasing containers with various colors helps to categorize foods. Meats, vegetables, fruits, mixed meals, and more can each then be color coded for easy access. Every container should be labeled for content and storage date.

Tea sieve

A tea sieve is used to hold herbs and other small flavorings separate from the main foods. If there are woody pieces or stems, the sieve will retain them so that the baby cannot accidentally eat them and choke. Parents should be cautious about foods that may choke a baby, particularly under age two.

Other items

Probably you already have the other necessary items in your kitchen. If not, add them as the need arises. Inspect your kitchen equipment and plan. Review the list of equipment in this section and note those items which are already in your kitchen.

STORING BABY FOODS

Wonderful storage containers to freeze baby foods are available in grocery stores and specialty stores. They come in convenient sizes and colors.

Most mothers find that four-ounce containers with lids, or plastic ice cube trays are most convenient. Ice cube trays allow you simply to pop out one or two cubes as needed. If you use these trays you should cover them with plastic wrap and tape them. It is important to freeze all foods in vapor and moisture proof containers with headroom for expansion of the foods.

Use containers that can go straight from the freezer to the microwave. If you select containers with different colors you can color code your storage. As an example, all meats might be stored in pink containers, vegetables in blue, fruits in clear, etc.

Label the item stored and the date stored so that you are certain that the baby's food is safe. We suggest that you limit food storage time in the freezer to thirty days, and either use it or throw it away before that time. Do not freeze or store beets, carrots, or spinach for babies under six months. Nitrates in these foods may change and become harmful.

Do not leave foods standing out of the refrigerator at room temperature to defrost. (Read the next section on warming and heating baby foods for the proper method.)

WARMING BABY FOODS

This book aims to avoid as many risks as possible, but we recognize that the age of microwave is here. We certainly know there is a controversy regarding the dangers of standing close to microwaves and we personally do not recommend using them when a baby is nearby. In addition, the heat is not always distributed evenly throughout foods when they are heated in a microwave. If you do choose to microwave, be very cautious about stirring the foods completely and testing the temperature before serving the baby.

Defrost frozen foods in the refrigerator. We suggest heating baby foods to "mildly warm." Many foods that adults prefer heated are just as acceptable to babies unheated.

Taking the chill off or warming can be accomplished by placing the food in a temperature-safe small dish. Place the dish in a pan of hot water until the food is the desired temperature. Egg poachers also work well. If you were lucky enough to receive a warmer/serving dish for a shower gift, that is another option for warming baby foods.

When babies are used to the temperature of mother's milk, they will expect beverages and first foods to be about that temperature. Mother's milk is basically body temperature; it should not feel either hot or cold when placed on your skin. Eating is certainly a nurturing time and making it pleasant for the baby is our objective.

TIME TO CLEAN UP!

Babies love to make up games that result in mothers cleaning, so don't be surprised when your baby starts dropping things from his feeding tray. Always testing, it almost seems that baby brains follow a law: "What I throw down, mother picks up." The thrower usually has a beguiling smile that goes along with this sport. Every mother has said, "If you throw it down one more time, I'm going to leave it there." But, who can stay annoyed when those five little teeth twinkle into a smile?

NONSLIP MATS FOR THE FLOOR

Stores now carry nonslip mats for the floor around the baby's feeding area. The theory is that it is easier to pick the mat up and clean it on a counter than to bend over and clean the floor. We agree wholeheartedly.

HAVE A TOWEL HANDY

The baby is learning to hold a cup. The moment is thrilling, but before he gets the hang of it you can expect several "wipe ups." Having a towel in close range before you start feeding makes things easier. Before feeding the baby, hang a towel on the back of a near-by chair so that you (but not the baby) can reach it, as needed. Also, you don't have to leave the baby to go get something for cleaning. While you are gone, he'll probably do it again.

Babies may feel mad about not being able to hold on to that slippery glass. Make him feel good about trying. "Whoops," and a smile so that he doesn't feel worse is supportive. Wouldn't you have liked consolation when you scraped the paint on the new car? Accidents can't be helped.

BUYING EASY-TO-CLEAN FURNITURE

When you are looking at furniture, strollers, playpens, swings, or other baby items, think about how easy or hard it will be to clean. High chairs or feeding tables should have as few areas in which food can become entrapped as possible. One of our favorite tables was made of a molded plastic material. There were no metal edges or corners for food to stick in; all edges were rounded and of one piece. Food and other soil will be around almost every item that the baby uses, so it is important to consider how an item will be cleaned before you buy it.

Moms and toddlers can clean together. It's good practice. Three and four year olds may not contribute much to cleaning but it is extremely important to encourage their efforts. Even eighteen-month-old babies will enjoy helping.

BABY CLOTHES AND FOOD

Buy bibs or aprons with sleeves and pockets to catch dropping food. Plastic is more effective than cloth. These items will be used until age two or more, so we suggest buying something big enough to allow for your baby's growth.

DISPOSABLE WIPES

Wipes are among the best inventions ever made for mothers. Keep them in the car, in the kitchen, and always within easy reach. A box tucked into the stroller is an excellent idea. Use not only to clean the obvious soil, but as a sanitary measure when out in public. Handling money, touching door knobs, and other public contacts can bring germs to the baby. Keep your own hands clean using wipes when soap and water aren't available.

TRASH BAGS

Folded, trash bags take up very little room. Without question these are about the most important "make your life easy" items around. Here are some places to stow them: in the car, in your handbag, in the stroller, by the feeding table. Traveling requires several. Restaurant dining requires at least one also. What will go into these trash bags? Soiled clothing, trash, diapers, and more.

A rather new item is an inflatable potty chair. It is soft on the baby's adorable little bottom. You can place a plastic bag in the center of this inflatable potty and wrap it over the outside. Simply remove it when the baby has used it. This is much easier and more sanitary than public rest rooms and very handy when you are out. Simply deflate it and it will take up very little space in your tote, and requires no cleanup.

CRAYON GRAFFITI

Today's scribblers may be tomorrow's Picassos, so why squelch talent? Tape butcher paper along the lower areas of the walls. If your toddler creates something spectacular, you can save it for posterity. Cut off special art and save with child's name, date, and age.

*2

First Step:
Foods For 0–6 Months

FROM NURSING TO FOOD

Mothers today are more knowledgeable about breast feeding. The health benefits and nurturing benefits for the breast-fed baby are causing more and more mothers to choose this option.

Sometimes it is not possible for mothers to nurse. Others begin by breast-feeding, and convert to formula because of work schedules or finding that expressing mother's milk in advance of feeding is too difficult.

Whatever you have chosen, how much formula or mother's milk your baby is accepting daily is an indication of his readiness to begin with starter foods. (See the section *When Is It Time to Start Baby Foods?* on page 19.)

Because the baby is used to sucking, and has not developed sufficiently to control where the food goes in his mouth, the first food feedings will be fluid enough to pour from a spoon. They should not, however, be fed from a bottle.

Matching the temperature of mother's milk will make the first feedings more pleasant, and a soft, covered spoon will make the change from mother's nipple more acceptable.

15

When food feedings begin, your baby may have a decreased desire for breast-feeding. If you have been nursing until now, you may wish to express some of your milk to mix with the baby's first foods. You will be adding some fluid to beginning foods, so either formula, water, or breast milk can be used.

If the baby is initially resistant to food, don't force the issue. Babies know when they are ready for the next stage in food and will likely let you know.

WATER

Formula or mother's milk usually provides enough fluids for an infant before he has been introduced to foods. But as the baby develops into a "food eater," he will want more water.

You may offer your baby water in a bottle occasionally, particularly during hot weather. Babies can dehydrate like anyone else. Water is not a substitute for formula or breast-feeding; it doesn't offer the necessary nutritional benefits.

Water may be added to pure and unsweetened juices as they are first introduced to the baby. By diluting the juice, the baby is getting a smaller amount of the new juice in each serving and adverse reactions can be observed prior to giving him full strength. One part juice and three parts water is a good mix, limiting the new juice to one ounce in a four-once serving. After you are assured that the new juice is well accepted by your baby, you may gradually decrease the water until the baby is getting full-strength juice.

Often babies like going to sleep while sucking on a bottle. Water is the best bottle filler to take to bed. When fruit juices, milk, or formula are given in bed, the baby will retain some of the fluid in pools around his teeth or gums. This practice is apt to cause tooth decay. Water solves the problem.

BABIES WILL ONLY DRINK WHEN THEY ARE THIRSTY

Many factors make our water sources less than favorable. When we look to the skies and see gray industrial dirt, we are seeing the makings of acid rain, and water that has contaminants. If we could look down into the layers of earth and see the chemicals that have leached into our water, more concerns would arise.

Pesticides and industrial waste will be working their way into our water systems for many years. What we do today will affect our water six and seven years from now.

Plumbing can contribute to the lead in your water. Even though the government is trying to regulate plumbing materials to avoid the lead problem, it will take years before our water is all lead free. So what is a parent to do? The best solution at present is to use bottled waters or install a filter on your water faucet. Don't switch off between the two, since changing water can change the balance of a baby's delicate little digestive system. If you decide that your baby will be drinking a commercially bottled water, just take it with you when you are away from home.

FIND OUT ABOUT THE WATER SOURCES IN YOUR AREA AND HAVE YOUR HOUSEHOLD PLUMBING CHECKED. TALK WITH THE BABY'S PEDIATRICIAN.

FOOD CAUTION LIST
AGES: 0–2 YEARS

Babies under two years may not be able to eat the foods listed below without the **risk of choking or gagging.** There are many additional foods and items that could pose a problem, so you should be aware and cautious about what the baby can put in his mouth. Talk with your pediatrician about this matter.

- Hot dogs
- Popcorn
- Nuts
- Raisins
- Skins on fruits and vegetables
- Grapes, olives, and other round foods
- Raw carrots and celery
- Seeds from produce or strings from vegetables
- Pieces of hard or overly chewy candy

Foods that should be offered with special discretion, (not under eighteen months), that are **difficult to digest** or that may cause other problems are:

- Chocolate
- Vanilla (with alcohol content)
- Honey
- Cucumbers
- Cabbage
- Cooked dry beans and baked beans
- Corn
- Uncooked onions

All foods should be preapproved by your baby's doctor before starting your infant on them.

WHEN IS IT TIME TO START BABY FOODS?

Your baby's doctor will recommend starting baby foods based on many factors:

• Age and overall development
• Weight gain and increased height
• Number of times nursing each day
• Number of ounces taken from a bottle each day
• Increased hunger
• Other factors determined by baby's doctor

Determining when to start baby foods depends on the individual needs of your child and your doctor's recommendations. The doctor will be watching your baby's weight gain as well as noting his age and activity growth. You may be asked to report how many times a day the baby is nursing or how many ounces of formula he or she consumes each day.

Many babies will begin eating starter foods when they have doubled their birth weight, at approximately thirteen or fourteen pounds. If your baby needs more than mother's milk or formula, the baby will probably let you know because he is getting hungry oftener. Breast-feeding may have increased to ten times a day. If the baby drinks from bottles, the intake may be in excess of four, eight-ounce bottles a day.

FEEDING TIME IS PRECIOUS

ALLERGIES

This is a book garnered from experience, talking with mothers and doctors, and a lot of observation. We are passing on what we have encountered in the twenty-five years since we started feeding the first baby in our household.

We do believe that children's performance in school and in general can be tremendously affected by what they eat. For that reason we hope that you will be alert to your baby's responses to foods.

Make a family chart of all foods that have affected family members with an allergic reaction. Discuss this history with your doctor when he is suggesting foods for your baby to try.

Allergic reactions have a broad range of symptoms. You may observe rashes, diarrhea, stomach ailments, pain, cramps, fussiness, or loose bowels. If you notice any unusual response after feeding a new food, immediately discontinue feeding that food and check with your doctor. You cannot assume that it is the food; the baby may be experiencing some other physical problem.

Each new food should be fed for a week, in small quantities, during which time you should not introduce any other new food.

There are some foods such as egg whites, milk products, or wheat that may be a problem when fed too early and yet could be accepted later on. This information is only to prompt you to be alert and to work with your doctor. The issue of allergies is too important to make determinations on your own.

In addition to keeping an eye out for allergies, foods that you buy from the store, including formulas, should be checked for age dating. One of my babies began vomiting at about four months. The doctor gave me instructions to follow, with the assumption that she was ill since no foods had been fed yet, and the formula had been given many times with no adverse reaction. The vomiting stopped, and the first time that the baby was given formula after the "illness" she started severe vomiting again. The formula cans were checked, and apparently the store had been selling outdated formula. Never assume food allergy or an illness, and always discuss products that have been fed with your doctor.

BASIC FOOD LIST

Review this list and inform your baby's doctor if there is a family history of allergic reaction to any of these foods. Discuss your baby's introduction to these foods or mixtures of these foods.

VEGETABLES
Asparagus
Artichokes
Baked beans
Carrots
Corn
Dried beans
Green beans
Green onions
Peas
Potatoes
Radishes
Spinach
Squash, summer

VEGETABLES (cont.)
Squash, yellow
Squash, zucchini
Sweet potatoes
Tomatoes
Yams

FRUITS
Apricots
Apples
Cantaloupe
Cherries
Grapefruit

FRUITS (cont.)
Grapes
Honeydew
Kiwis
Loquats
Nectarines
Oranges
Peaches
Pears
Pineapple
Plums
Strawberries
Tangerines
Watermelon

DRIED FRUITS
Prunes
Raisins

FISH
Cod
Crabmeat
Halibut
Lobster
Orange roughy
Perch
Salmon
Shrimp
Sole fillet
Trout
Tuna

POULTRY
Chicken
Liver
Turkey

MEATS
Bacon
Beef
Ham
Lamb
Pork
Veal

*CEREALS &
FLOURS*
Barley
Corn
Oatmeal
Rice
Wheat
Graham

*MILK
PRODUCTS*
Butter
Buttermilk
Cheddar cheese
Cottage cheese
Milk
Monterey Jack
  cheese
Parmesan cheese
Swiss cheese
Whipped cream
Yogurt

EGGS
Egg yolks
  (cooked)
Whole eggs
  (cooked)
Raw eggs

GELATINS

BOUILLON

SOY SAUCE

*HERBS AND
  SPICES*
Allspice
Basil
Bayleaf
Cinnamon
Garlic
Garlic salt
Nutmeg
Oregano
Pepper
Salt

*PEANUT
  BUTTER*

HONEY

CORN STARCH

KNOWING YOUR VEGETABLES AND FRUITS INSIDE AND OUT

There are many chemicals found on the inside and outside of fruits and vegetables.

• Pesticides
• Fungicides
• Herbicides
• Rodenticides

Parents must assume that they may be feeding their babies hazardous materials if measures are not taken to select organic produce.

To protect your baby:
• Thoroughly wash or peel all produce.
• Look for foods that are labeled "organically grown."
• Ask your merchants which crops are grown in the United States. Avoid foreign produce from countries such as Mexico, where chemical use is less restrictive than in the United States.

FRESHNESS AND IRRADIATION

Irradiation alters produce that has been so exposed. Enzymes are changed and hence the nutritional benefits are changed.

Produce is irradiated to extend shelf life, which reduces product cost by decreasing spoilage, and allows more time for packing and storing. Time will tell in regard to long-term effects on our health.

The government requires that signs indicate when produce has been irradiated. Once again, call the buyer of your supermarket chain or ask the produce manager to point irradiated produce out for you.

Many areas have farmers' markets that sell their wares once a week. Usually farmers who have grown the produce are present so that you can ask them questions about how the fruits and vegetables have been grown.

Larger cities, in particular, often have specialty stores for either health foods or good produce.

If you are buying from a store that receives produce the day it is picked, you can probably shop once a week and maintain the foods in good condition until the following week's shopping. Use the most perishable fruits and vegetables first.

BUY ORGANIC FRUITS AND VEGETABLES AVOID CHEMICALS AND IRRADIATION . . .

Symptoms of Overexposure to Chemicals:

- Rashes
- Dizziness
- Nausea
- Diarrhea
- Bleeding skin
- Yellow skin
- Hair loss
- Brain lesions
- Various forms of cancer

YOU WILL BE AMAZED AT THE IMPROVED FLAVOR WHEN YOU SELECT YOUR FRUITS AND VEGETABLES WITH CARE.

THE VERY FIRST FEEDINGS

The first spoon should have a long handle and a soft covering. Regular spoons are hard and cold to the touch. The covered spoon will be more comfortable during the transition. Even though the first foods will be quite liquid, never feed them from a bottle. The baby is ready to learn about taking food from a spoon instead of sucking from a nipple or bottle.

LITTLE MOUTHS NEED LITTLE SPOONS

Beginning the feeding of baby foods is a slow process. At first you will give the baby a small portion of food. He will probably play with it, try to spit it out, suck or clamp his mouth around the spoon, and perhaps turn his head away. You can play a little while but don't stay with it too long. Another day you can try again.

The readiness to try first foods is all up to the baby. Don't coax or pressure the baby to eat. Feeding time will soon become a pleasure to both mother and baby.

IT IS TIME FOR SMILES AND BONDING
MAKE AN INVESTMENT IN LOVE

BABY'S FIRST FOODS

When your baby is four to six months old you will probably be hearing coos and gurgles and getting big smiles. Maybe you'll see some adorable front teeth.

When this "first foods" period begins, it will take about thirteen weeks to try all the beginning foods. Since doctors'

instructions are widely varied, some babies will be given
foods at four months while many will not. Introduce new
foods carefully, no more than one each week.

New food list for your doctor's approval

For your convenience, we have listed the most commonly suggested foods for this time period on the next
page. You can take this list with you when the baby has a
checkup. As the doctor approves each item, make a note
of the date in your book. On the following page you can
make notes about the baby's response to each new food
item. We cannot stress enough that if the baby shows any
signs of allergic reaction, you should stop feeding that food
and immediately tell your doctor.

If your baby has a sitter, share the information to make
certain that he does not feed foods to your baby that cause
problems. Keeping notes will assist you in making the information clear and understood.

How to Thin Foods

These foods will be blended and mixed with either water,
cooking juices, fruit juice, formula, or mother's milk.

YOU SHOULD BE ABLE TO POUR
THESE FIRST FOODS FROM A SPOON

How Much Do I Feed?

The first time you try a new food, only feed one spoonful. If the baby likes it and there are no adverse reactions,
you will increase the amount at the next feeding. If your
baby indicates that he has had enough, do not coax him to
eat more.

Remember that foods left over from the feeding should

not be stored, so keep the initial portions small. If the baby's feeding spoon has been in the food at serving time, bacteria may grow if you store the leftovers.

BEGINNING FOODS

Fruits
Bananas
Apples
Pears
Peaches
Prunes

Cereals
Single grain baby cereals
as selected by your doctor
Rice
Barley
Oatmeal

Vegetables
Peas
Carrots
Green Beans
Squash
Sweet Potatoes

Fluids
Mother's Milk
Formula
Water

Dilute selected fruit juices: prune, apple, or pear (do not serve citrus juice to this age group). Often doctors recommend first servings of juices when the baby begins to drink from a cup. Check with your pediatrician.

CEREALS

Both mother and baby are adjusting to a new regime. For your convenience and with the baby's nutritional needs in mind, we suggest that you use commercially prepared baby cereal at this time. In the beginning you will be feeding such a small amount that it is not worth making your own.

Baby rice cereal is often thought to be the most easily digested of the commercial cereals on the market. As time goes by, you will probably try most of the available flavors. Babies like to try new foods slowly and when your doctor says to go forth, you may be also serving barley cereal and oatmeal. Single grains are best at this time. Gradually, you will add fruit to them and finally you will be mixing grains.

Baby's instant rice cereal from the local supermarket can be mixed with mother's milk, formula, or water. Use the package instructions for mixing unless your doctor has special recommendations. Generally, the first time you try the cereal you will mix one teaspoon of cereal to five teaspoons of water.

The mixture of cereal for four-to-six-month-old babies must be very runny. Each day, your baby will probably eat a little more until he is eating about three or four tablespoons per serving.

JUICES

We believe that buying commercially prepared baby juices during the four-to-six-month period makes sense. We have taken into account three factors. The primary factor is nutrition, and commercial juices are just fine. The other two factors, money and time, have also been considered.

The four-ounce serving sizes (one serving) are convenient when you take the baby out. They should not be opened until you are prepared to serve them, and anything that the baby doesn't drink must be immediately refrigerated or thrown out.

Apple juice and pear juice are popular at this time. If the

baby takes to the juice, it can be used as the fluid in preparing baby cereal.

There are mixed flavored juices and single flavored juices. During these first months, the single flavors are preferable. Juices, as well as foods, must be tried for a week as the only new food during that week. If the baby accepts pureed and cooked apples, most likely apple juice will also be well accepted.

At a later time, we will suggest making your own juices. Fresh juices are often so popular with the family that they become a healthy habit for the entire family.

FRUITS

Bananas

Your little hand blender is probably the easiest to use since bananas are soft and you are making single servings. Select a ripe, soft banana. Cut the banana in half, only peeling the half you will use. Cover the unused half with plastic wrap, pressing out any air and save in the refrigerator.

Fresh Banana Blend

Blend a half banana, adding either your baby's formula or drinking water, until smooth and the appropriate consistency for your baby's stage of development. New babies like an almost fluid consistency; however, soon the baby will accept bananas without added fluids.

BANANA AND CEREAL

¼ banana
1 serving dry baby cereal
Baby formula or drinking water, as needed

Prepare the baby's cereal as per package instructions. Mash the banana and mix thoroughly with prepared cereal. These very first feedings must pour from a spoon.

AH! APPLESAUCE

2 pounds cooking apples
1 squeeze lemon juice

To avoid adding sugar, talk with your produce manager to obtain a sweet variety of apple.

Wash, peel, and core two pounds of cooking apples.

Rinse apples again. Cut and slice. Place in a two-quart pan, and cover with water. Bring to a boil, and cover the pan. Reduce heat, and let simmer for 10 minutes. Test the apples with a fork. Continue cooking until tender. Fork should run through easily.

Drain the apples, saving the cooking juice. For applesauce that will be stored, add a few drops of lemon juice to the cooking juices before pouring in the blender. A drop or two of lemon juice will help apple sauce retain its color. Place the apples in a blender. Blend and add the cooking juices until the appropriate smooth texture is attained.

Cool and place in an ice cube tray. Freeze. You may

remove the cubes as needed and heat as you would any baby food in a sauce pan with a top. Serving at room temperature is also acceptable.

Makes ten ¼-cup servings.

PEARS

2 cups pears
1 squeeze lemon juice
⅔ cup water

Thoroughly wash, peel, and core pears. Rinse again. Bring water and pears to a boil in a sauce pan. Reduce the heat and simmer. Test with a fork for tenderness after 10 to 15 minutes.

Blend pears, adding natural cooking juices as needed for smooth texture and so that mixture will pour from a spoon. Add a drop or two of lemon juice to the fluid if you desire to prevent discoloration of fruit.

Cool and spoon into an ice cube tray. Freeze. You may remove the cubes as needed and heat as you would any baby food in a sauce pan with a top. Serving at room temperature is also acceptable.

Makes 10 servings.

PEACHES, PLUMS, OR APRICOTS

2 cups peaches, plums, or apricots
⅔ cup boiling water
Formula, milk, fruit juice, or cooking water as
   required to make a smooth blend

Follow directions for pears (page 31). When selecting fresh
fruit, be certain that the fruit is ripened sufficiently to make
sweet, flavorful food for baby. Most fruits will ripen when
placed in a sunny area of the kitchen for a day or two.

    When fruits are out of season, or are not ripened suffi-
ciently, frozen fruits may be used as a replacement. Add
formula, milk, fruit juice, or water as required to make a
smooth blend.

    Canned, unsweetened peaches may be pureed. First wash
the peach halves under cold water.

Makes 10 servings.

PRUNES

2 stewed prunes
4 tablespoons baby formula

Use stewed and pitted prunes in jars from your supermarket. Be sure they are pitted. Prunes tend to be laxative and
should be served in small quantities. Blending prunes with
the baby's formula will produce a sweet and nutritious fruit
blend. Put blended prunes through a colander to remove

any skin particles. Blend prunes and formula. Be certain to get your doctor's approval before serving prunes.

Note: Dried prunes may be used by soaking until soft and stewing. They will require simmering for about 30 minutes to become soft and plump. Remove the pits.

Makes 3 servings.

VEGETABLES

PEAS

1 cup shelled peas
Water or formula as needed

Fresh peas can be wonderful. Open one pod and try the peas inside before you buy. They should be sweet and tender. If the pods look dried or molding, don't buy. Frozen peas are an acceptable alternative.

When cooking fresh peas, shell and rinse peas. Cover peas with boiling water in pot. Cook until tender, about 10 to 12 minutes.

Place drained peas in blender, add cooking water or formula as needed to make smooth consistency that will pour from a spoon. Blend. Fill ice cube tray, cover, and freeze. For serving, remove from freezer and heat as any baby food. (See pages 9–11 for storage and warming of baby foods.)

Makes 10 servings.

CARROTS

Check with your pediatrician before introducing carrots. Do not use the carrot juice at this early age.

2 carrots
Water as needed

Peel and wash carrots.
Cut carrots in ½-inch rounds, and place in pan. Cover with water, bring to a boil, and cook with lid on pot for about 10 minutes.

Test with a fork for tenderness. Drain.

Place carrots in blender and blend, adding water until consistency is smooth and fluffy. Carrots must be liquid enough to pour from a spoon.

To store, spoon carrot puree into an ice cube tray. Freeze.

** Do not let carrots sit at room temperature.

Makes 10 servings.

SQUASH
(Butternut or acorn varieties)

1 Butternut or acorn squash
Water or formula as needed for consistency

Set the oven at 350 degrees. Thoroughly wash the outside of the squash. Cut squash in half and remove the seeds and pulp. Place upside down in a baking pan and cook for 30 minutes. Next, turn the squash halves so that the cut side is up. Cover the squash with foil and bake an additional 25 minutes. Test with fork for tenderness.

Cool, and then scoop the squash from its shell. Place in blender. Blend, adding formula or drinking water to bring to proper consistency. Squash must pour from the spoon. It may be necessary to press through a colander to remove strings and pulp.

Fill ice cube tray, and cover. Freeze. May be served at room temperature or heated.

Butternut squash makes 8 servings.
Acorn squash makes 4 servings.

GREEN BEANS

¾ pound green beans
Water, as needed for cooking

Wash beans thoroughly. Remove ends, pulling side strings off in the process. Cut beans, then place in a sauce pan and cook in 1-½ inches of boiling water. Reduce heat. Cover, and cook for 25 minutes. Test with a fork for tenderness.

Blend, adding cooking juices as needed, for smooth consistency. Beans should be liquefied enough to pour from a spoon.

Store in ice cube trays, and cover. Freeze.

Makes 10 servings.

SWEET POTATOES

2 small sweet potatoes (1 pound total)
Apple juice, as needed for consistency

Baked and Blended
Wash sweet potatoes, cut off the ends, and puncture. Bake
at 425 degrees for 30 to 45 minutes, depending on the size
of the potato, until a fork easily goes through the potato.
Scoop out the sweet potato and blend with fruit juice for
appropriate consistency.

Stovetop cooking
If you prefer stovetop cooking, you can boil the sweet potatoes. Wash sweet potatoes thoroughly. Cut off the ends.

Place sweet potatoes in a pot of boiling water. Cook for
approximately 35 minutes. Potatoes vary in size and so will
your cooking time. Cook until tender. Remove from heat
and drain. Peel.

Put sliced sweet potatoes in a blender. If you choose to
peel the potatoes before cooking, which takes longer than
peeling after cooking, you can use the cooking juices. If
you cook with skins on, we recommend using formula,
mother's milk, or water to get the proper consistency for
your baby. Blend at high speed until smooth.

Cool briefly and place in cube molds in your freezer
container.

Steaming
Clean sweet potatoes, cut off ends, and peel. Cut in slices
and place in a fine mesh steamer basket. Steam, using a
small amount of water, until tender. Store as usual.

Makes 10 servings.

3

Second Step:
Foods for 6–12 Months

Check all new foods and textures with your baby's doctor before trying them.

This section covers the ages between six and twelve months or after your baby has been introduced to approximately twelve new foods. Since each baby develops at a different rate, no book can tell you exactly when your baby is ready for a change in the texture of his food. You and your doctor will evaluate your baby and make food and texture choices.

If a short-handled, fat-bowled baby spoon is available, the baby may try to spoon his own food. His coordination is likely not good enough to really be self-feeding. Trial comes before perfection. Let him play; he is learning to find his mouth!

The period from six months to twelve months is a time for big change. As you work your way through the recipes, some will be acceptable at six months while others will be best tried near the end of the twelfth month. Each food must still be tried individually.

Don't rush to try every new food in this section. Your baby has a lifetime to experience and enjoy new foods.

Sixth and Seventh Months

By six months, many babies are learning how to transfer food around in their mouths. Some teeth are most likely present. Your baby will be trying to put anything within his grasp into his mouth. You are witnessing the beginning skills needed for self-feeding. Some babies will be able to bring the rim of a glass to their mouth. Drinking from a cup is on its way! Despite all of this development, the changes in texture and liquefication of baby's food will be moderate. At this age the foods will still pour from a spoon.

Eighth Month

Around the eighth month, some babies are beginning to try chewing. The chewing motion does not indicate that he is accomplishing much. A lot of "gumming" goes on before the molars actually take over.

Ninth through Twelfth Months

In months nine through twelve, many babies are ready for the following:

• Finely minced foods mixed with pureed foods
• Mashed, soft foods
• Foods containing a few small, soft lumps

FOOD LIST FOR TRIAL DURING 6–12 MONTH PERIOD

Discuss which foods to give your baby with the baby's doctor. The list will assist you in checking off each item and the date introduced. We have used mild seasonings and herbs in some foods for babies over ten months, but that issue should be decided by your doctor as opinions about these additions vary. Follow his advice.

VEGETABLES	FRUITS (cont.)	DAIRY (cont.)
Asparagus	Papayas	Egg yolks
Beets	Passion fruit	Mild cheeses
Corn	Peaches	Milk
Creamed corn	Pineapple	Natural yogurt
Green beans	Plums	
Mushrooms		JUICES
Spinach	MEATS, FISH,	Non-citrus, made
Squash	AND POULTRY	from fruits the
Sweet potatoes	Beef	baby has success-
Tomatoes	Chicken	fully tried. Clari-
White potatoes	Ham	fied; no seeds or
Yams	Lamb	pulp.
	Liver	
FRUITS	Pork	OTHER
Apples	Turkey	Gelatin
Apricots	Veal	Simple sauces
Bananas	White fish	
Guavas		GRAIN
Kiwis	DAIRY	Pastas
Mangoes	Cottage cheese	Rice

CEREALS

During the baby's first few months we recommended feeding commercial baby cereals. The next step is to check the list of cereals below with your doctor and begin to make your own dry cereal from adult cereals. We found that an electric chopper/grinder was convenient for this process. It makes small amounts quickly and easily.

A little oatmeal in the chopper/grinder is changed into a fine cereal for your baby in seconds. If you prefer to make larger batches for future use, a blender can be used. Store the dry cereal in an airtight container.

Babies frequently are started on rice cereal followed by oat, wheat, corn, and barley cereals. Single grain cereals are fed during the first months and cereals in combinations may be introduced around the seventh or eighth month. As new foods are offered, cereals can be mixed with fruit purees, and later with egg yolks.

Texture and type of cereals should be introduced as your doctor recommends for your baby. The baby may show signs that he is not ready for a particular food; he may seem fussy, appear to have stomach discomfort, such as gas, or have changes in his bowel movements.

The varieties of cereals are numerous and some of them are listed below:

- Jars of prepared baby cereal
- Dry baby cereals: rice, oat, barley, wheat
- Oatmeal
- Cream of Rice
- Cream of Wheat
- Cereal flakes: rice, barley, wheat, rye

Cooking directions are on packages. You may either grind the dry cereals for appropriate texture or cook them first before blending. Either way, you must be certain that there are no particles that could result in the baby's choking. The textures, after fluids such as milk or formula have been added, should never be tacky. Textures will be quite fluid at first and will drop easily from a spoon for babies under a year.

EAGER FOR EGG YOLKS?

Your baby may be six, eight, ten months or even a year when your doctor suggests that you try eggs. He will probably have you try the yolks first. Given at too early an age, egg whites may produce an allergic reaction with babies whose digestive systems are not fully developed.

Preparation of the egg

Wash the egg shell with cool water. Cover the egg with water in a small sauce pan. Bring the water to a boil and turn the heat down. Simmer the egg for fifteen minutes.

Remove the egg with a slotted spoon and run cold water over it. Now you can easily remove the shell.

First egg yolk trial

Try a small amount of mashed egg yolk mixed with formula, milk or a fluid that the baby drinks regularly. Increase the amount of egg yolk gradually, and watch for reactions.

Ways to include egg yolks in foods:

- Puree egg yolk with green vegetable puree (see page 53)
- Puree egg yolk with baby cereal and fluid
- Puree egg yolk with fruit and cereal
- Puree egg yolk with sauce and pasta

When your baby is ready for zwieback, mash egg yolk with natural yogurt and use it as a spread.

YOGURT

Natural yogurt is a springboard for many food combinations. The natural creamy texture and bland flavor allows it to blend nicely with a variety of foods.

Opinions vary about when babies should be introduced to yogurt. Yogurt is a milk product and children with allergies or sensitivity to milk may not use yogurt. Talk with your doctor about starting this food. It is usually easily digested if there are no problems with milk.

Until the first year is up, we suggest cooking all fruits and vegetables, with the exception of bananas. Raw fruits and vegetables, as well as citrus, berries, and dried fruits are often better introduced sometime after the first birthday. At that time, yogurt can be mixed with raw foods.

Yogurt and Fruits

Mix natural yogurt and fruit purees in equal proportions. There are many good combinations. Here are some fruits and fruit combinations that babies seem to enjoy blended with yogurt:

- Applesauce
- Apricots
- Peaches
- Bananas
- Pears
- Prune Molé mixed with baby rice cereal

- Apples and raisin molé
- Apricots and pineapple
- Peaches and graham cracker crumbs
- Bananas and apples
- Pears and raisin molé

If you are not storing your own purees, you may use canned or frozen fruits. Be certain that you buy fruits that are designated as "natural pack," avoiding sugar and additives. If necessary, rinse fruit packed in sugar under cold water.

FRUITS

Cooked and Fresh Fruits

Many changes will take place between the sixth and twelfth months. Crawling and walking and lots of curiosity abound. Each new food flavor and texture will bring facial expressions that you cannot decipher. Discuss which fruits your baby is ready to try with your baby's doctor and watch that little baby make faces.

Inhaling or choking is always a consideration, so skins and seeds must be removed. When a colander for pressing or straining is suggested, we recommend the cone-shaped style rather than the round version. The wooden cone-shaped presser that accompanies the colander is effective in pressing pulpy materials.

Canned Peaches and Pears

When peaches and pears or other favorite fruits are not in season, the canned varieties are quite acceptable. To avoid sugar, purchase the products that are labeled "natural" or "unsweetened." If you are compelled to use a fruit that has been packed in heavy syrup, rinse the syrup off of the fruit under cold water. Most fruits will have enough fluid content that a suitable puree can be made without adding more fluid, however, if more fluid is needed, any fruit juice that your baby has successfully tried will work. The easiest fluid addition is always drinking water.

Bananas

Ripe bananas pureed are enjoyed by themselves or used as a natural sweetener in other recipes.

Fresh Peaches, Plums, and Apricots

Select ripe fruit or ripen before use. Exposing unripened fruit to sunlight will usually ripen fruit in a day or two. In some cases, the fruit has been picked too early and will not ripen satisfactorily before spoiling. Checking the color of fruit at the stem base, select that which has the least green coloration.

Wash, remove pits, and steam until tender, using a small amount of water in the bottom of the pan.

Press through a colander to remove skins. Puree, or, later on, you may serve it as it is after pressing through the colander. Probably, using the colander alone will be acceptable at about seven months. Check with your baby's doctor. For a more liquid texture, add water.

When your doctor indicates that the baby can eat small pieces of fruit as finger food, it is imperative that you supervise.

Canned Pineapple

Select unsweetened canned pineapple and use a blender to prepare the appropriate texture. Pineapple is another excellent sweetener which will enhance other foods. Save the juice for future use. Do not store it in the can, though; use a sealable plastic container dish.

Applesauce

As you make your own applesauce (page 30) you can gradually allow a bit more texture and lumps as your child is ready for them.

Stewed Prunes

Prepared the same as recipe on page 146, pitted prunes must be pressed through the colander to remove the skins. Prunes are excellent natural sweeteners mixed in small quantities with other foods.

Melons, Mangoes, Guavas, and Kiwis

Wash all fruits before you begin to prepare them and remove the seeds, cores, and rinds. As your baby approaches his first birthday, you can ask your doctor about feeding him pieces of soft fruits. Until your doctor approves fresh fruits, cook and puree, or mash baby's fruits.

Citrus fruits and berries will be offered later. Some doctors may allow them just before the first year mark. We will include them in the next age bracket, 12–18 months.

COTTAGE CHEESE VARIATIONS

Check date on cottage cheese carton before purchasing. Freezing is not recommended for any cottage cheese mixtures.

Cottage Cheese and Fruit

Cooked fruits to mix with cottage cheese: peaches, pears, plums, apricots, and apples.

Unsweetened, canned pineapple is wonderful with cottage cheese and fast to prepare for impatient babies.

Bananas are sweet and usually well received by the younger set when mixed with cottage cheese.

Equal proportions of fruit and cottage cheese will give a good taste and texture. Blend or mash depending on the baby's development.

Cooking juices from fruit, apple juice, or unsweetened pineapple juice may be used to make the mix more fluid as required.

Cottage Cheese and Vegetables

Cottage cheese in equal parts with many vegetable purees will make a good, quick meal. Try any of the following vegetable purees for the mixture:

- Zucchini
- Spinach
- Green beans
- Beets
- Peas
- White potato
- Zucchini and summer squash

- Spinach and sauteed onions
- Green beans and minced ham
- Beets and orange juice
- Asparagus with Parmesan cheese

Yogurt and Vegetables

There are many combinations of vegetables and yogurt that will please your baby. You can experiment with your own combinations and try these suggestions. In the instance of certain rather strong flavored vegetables, we have suggested mixing them with sweet fruits. Your baby may like them all by themselves so don't prejudge. Try them alone first.

Pureed vegetables and vegetable combination suggestions to mix in equal portions with yogurt:

- Cauliflower
- Green beans
- Peas

- Carrots, with a small amount of raisin molé
- Beets and pineapple

- Spinach with a drop of lemon juice
- Brussels sprouts and apricots
- Cauliflower and apricots
- Green beans and minced turkey
- Peas and carrots

VEGETABLES

GREEN BEANS AND COTTAGE CHEESE

⅔ cup green beans
⅓ cup cottage cheese

Steam green beans, then remove, and puree in blender. Mix green bean puree and cottage cheese; blend until texture is appropriate for baby. Add cooking fluids from the beans as needed to make the blend more fluid.

Makes 2–4 servings.

GREEN BEANS AND APRICOTS

⅔ cup green bean puree
⅓ cup apricot puree

Mix together ⅔ green bean puree and ⅓ apricot puree. Serve or store in freezer.

Makes 4 servings.

GREEN BEANS, CARROTS, ZUCCHINI, AND POTATO

1 medium potato, cut in cubes
1 medium carrot, sliced in thin rounds
1 zucchini, cut in rounds (leaving outer skin on)
6 green beans, cut in 1-inch pieces
Milk, or vegetable cooking juices as needed for consistency

Boil potato for 20 minutes in a medium-sized pot. Add carrots to pot and continue cooking for 5 minutes.

Place zucchini and green beans in a steamer basket. Position the steamer basket over cooking potato and carrot, allowing the green beans and zucchini to steam for 10 minutes while the potato and carrot continue to cook.

Drain all vegetables, and store the cooking fluids. Puree the vegetable mixture in a blender. Add milk or vegetable cooking juices as desired.

As the baby grows older, you may wish to embellish this recipe by adding a touch of butter, a squeeze of lemon, and a sprinkle of chives.

Serve or store in freezer (leftovers may be stored in freezer as well). Ice cube trays with a plastic wrap cover are convenient for small serving sizes.

Makes 8–10 servings.

CARROT AND BANANA PUREE

1 carrot, steamed
½ ripe banana

Puree steamed carrot and ripe banana. Add cooking juices from the carrot, if required, for additional moisture. Serve. Mom will enjoy the extra serving for a snack. This is best enjoyed when it is first made, as the bananas will discolor if stored.

Makes 2 servings.

CARROT AND BROCCOLI PUREE

6 fresh broccoli flowerets
2 small carrots, cut in thin rounds

Steam broccoli flowerets and carrot slices in a steamer basket for about 15 minutes, until tender. Puree, adding cooking juices as desired. Store 1 day only in refrigerator.

For Adults:
Remove carrots and broccoli from the steamer pan after about 8 or 10 minutes. Vegetables should be crisp, firm, and tender. Serve with fine strips of red bell pepper. Mix a touch of garlic salt and lemon juice with melted butter. Drizzle this mixture over the vegetables and serve.

Makes 2 baby servings and 2 adult servings.

CARROT, APPLE, AND RAISIN PUREE

1 carrot, cut in thin rounds
1 sweet apple, cut in eighths
8 raisins, stewed (raisins must be pressed through
  colander before use in recipe)

Place carrot slices in a steamer tray and steam over water for 10 minutes.

Add apples to the steamer tray and continue steaming for 10 more minutes.

Remove, and puree in blender, adding raisins and cooking juices as required for appropriate texture.

After doctor approves spices, a pinch of cinnamon will add to the flavor of this dish.

Extra servings may be stored in the freezer. When storing, add a few drops of lemon juice and mix, to retain color.

Makes 4–6 servings.

BRUSSELS SPROUTS AND VEGETABLES

6 brussels sprouts, washed, with outer leaves trimmed
  away
6 baby carrots, washed thoroughly
1 green onion, cut in 1-inch pieces (for 11–12 month
  old)
¼ teaspoon dill weed, placed in a tea sieve

Place tea sieve in the water of a steamer pot.

Place other ingredients on the steamer rack and steam for 12 minutes or until tender.

Remove vegetables from rack, and blend, adding cooking juices as needed.

Serve or store in freezer. Use a covered freezer container.

For adults:
Increase amounts as desired. Serve with melted butter adding additional dill while melting.

Makes 8–10 servings.

CABBAGE AND RICE

1 tablespoon minced onion
1 teaspoon butter
1 small carrot, coarsely shredded
1 1-inch wedge cabbage, shredded
4 ounces precooked rice, warmed

Sauté onion in butter until translucent, then remove onion from skillet.

Steam carrot in a sauce pan for 5 minutes, using a strainer to contain shredded carrot.

Add shredded cabbage to strainer, and steam together for an additional 5 minutes. Let drain.

Heat rice, dipping it in hot water, using a strainer.

Blend cabbage, then add rice, carrots, and onion. Serve.

Makes 2–3 servings.

BAKED TOMATO

Tomatoes and bread crumbs made from wheat are both foods that some children will not tolerate. They may bring about an allergic reaction when served before the baby is ready for them. Try these near the 12th month, testing small quantities first.

1 large tomato
1 tablespoon minced onion
2 tablespoons seasoned bread crumbs
1 tablespoon butter

Sauté minced onion in butter until translucent. Mix in bread crumbs, stir, and set aside.

Wash and remove the stem from tomato. Cut the tomato horizontally in half. Place the two halves in a baking pan, cut side up. Spread the bread crumb mixture over the two tomato halves.

Bake at 400 degrees for 15 to 20 minutes. The crumbs will be golden brown and the tomato halves tender when they are done. Tomatoes vary in size and therefore should be checked after 10 to 12 minutes for doneness.

Puree tomato, adding water as needed. This will make a great food base mixed with other pureed vegetables, meats, chicken, pastas, or rice.

Serve or store in refrigerator and use the next day.

For adults:
Make additional tomatoes for adults. Mix chopped parsley and Parmesan cheese with the bread crumbs before baking and spread over tomato halves. Salt and pepper as desired.

Makes 2–3 servings.

ASPARAGUS PUREE

3 asparagus spears

Select thin, young asparagus. Wash and snap off coarse ends, about 1-inch from the bottom.

Cook in an asparagus steamer pan or steam basket, using a small amount of water, about ½-inch in the bottom of the pan.

Cooking time depends on the asparagus. Test at 5 and then at 10 minutes for tenderness.

Puree, using cooking juices as needed for additional moisture.

Options for older babies, (near the twelve month period):
Mix one tablespoon of mayonnaise, one egg yolk, and a dash of mustard into the puree. Later on, when asparagus is used as a finger food, the mayonnaise mixture can be used as a dip.

Serve or store in the refrigerator for not more than one day. Use the excess for adult finger food dip.

Makes 3–4 servings.

WHITE POTATOES

Potatoes can be baked, boiled, or steamed. Steaming retains nutrients best. It is faster to peel, cube, and boil than to bake. Also, it requires more energy to heat the oven than to use the stove top, unless you are already using it for additional baking.

Uses for Cooked Potatoes

Potatoes are wonderful natural thickeners. Strong flavored vegetables are often more acceptable to babies when mixed with the blander flavoring of white potatoes. Mashed potatoes are baby favorites when blended with a bit of butter and some milk. As the baby is developing, leave a few lumps in the mashed potato. This is an excellent food for introducing new textures.

BAKED POTATOES

Preheat the oven to 375 degrees.
  Scrub the outside peel of the potato.
  Make steam holes in several places with a fork.
  Brush cooking oil over the potato skin.
  Depending on the size of the potato, bake for an hour to an hour-and-a half. Mash with a fork or blend, depending on the texture required. Add milk if the baby needs less tacky texture.

One average sized potato makes 4–6 servings.

BOILED POTATOES

Scrub potato skins. Peel, and cube potatoes.

Place potatoes in a pan of boiling water and cover with a lid. When water returns to a boil, reduce heat and continue cooking for 20 minutes. Test for tenderness with a fork. Potatoes are done when the fork slides through easily. Mash or blend with milk.

STEAMED POTATOES

Prepare potato cubes as above. Place in a steam basket over water. Steam for about 20 minutes and test with a fork for tenderness.

BAKED EGGPLANT

Try this when baby is approaching his first birthday!

1 small eggplant
1 tablespoon parsley, finely chopped
2 tablespoons grated Parmesan cheese
½ cup bread crumbs
Mozzarella cheese (1 slice for each eggplant slice)
Tomato juice as needed for consistency
¼ cup all-purpose flour
2 eggs

Wash the eggplant and slice it into ½-inch thick rounds. Very lightly salt the slices, and place them on a rack for 25 minutes to drain. This lessens bitterness.

Mix together parsley, Parmesan cheese, and bread crumbs. Spread the mixture over a sheet of waxed paper.

Cover another sheet of waxed paper with flour.

Beat eggs in a bowl.

Coat both sides of eggplant with flour, and dip in the egg, then coat both sides with the bread crumb mixture.

Place each slice of eggplant, when coated, on a baking sheet.

Bake at 350 degrees for 30 minutes. Place a slice of mozzarella cheese on each eggplant slice, and bake for an additional 5 minutes, or until the cheese is bubbling and a fork slices through eggplant easily.

For baby, puree 1 small slice of eggplant, adding tomato juice as needed for consistency.

For adults:
Sauté garlic (one minced clove) in olive oil until translucent. Add diced tomatoes, and stir for a short time. Serve over eggplant slices.

Makes 1 baby serving and 4 adult servings.

OKRA, TOMATOES, AND GREEN BEANS

2 ½-inch slices okra
¼ baked tomato, medium-sized
2 tablespoons green bean puree
1 sprinkle Parmesan cheese

Wash and cut off okra stems. Boil for 15 minutes, then drain.

Puree okra, green bean puree, and baked tomato. Add Parmesan cheese to the puree for additional flavoring.

Makes 2–3 servings

Suggestions for adult servings:
Make larger quantities for use as a base in preparing soups. It is also tasty over pasta for a quick meal.

CAULIFLOWER, CELERY, AND PEAS IN SAUCE

6 cauliflower flowerets
2 celery stalks
¼ cup fresh peas
¼ cup cheddar cheese, grated

Wash cauliflower, removing leaves and stem. Break into flowerets. Store remaining flowerets for additional adult meals.

Clean celery and remove strings. Cut into short, thin slices.

Shell peas and rinse.

Using a steam tray over a small amount of water, steam peas for 5 minutes. Add cauliflower and celery. Continue to steam for 7 minutes, until tender.

Drain, and sprinkle grated cheddar cheese over hot vegetables to melt. Mash with a fork and serve. If your toddler will not readily accept the texture, blend. Refrigerate unserved portions up to 2 days or freeze.

Makes 6 servings.

CAULIFLOWER AND APRICOTS

½ cup steamed cauliflower
2 tablespoons apricot puree (homemade or commercial brand)

Puree steamed cauliflower, and mix in apricot puree for a sweet and tasty way to interest baby in cauliflower. Store second serving in refrigerator. Do not freeze food that has been frozen before.

Makes 2 servings.

LET'S PLAY SQUASH!

Squash Varieties:

- Banana squash
- Yellow squash
- Green table squash
- Butternut squash

- Summer squash
- Zucchini squash
- Spaghetti squash

GREEN TABLE SQUASH

1 green table squash
¼ cup sweet fruit puree (apricot or pineapple)
1 teaspoon butter

Bake green table squash at 375 degrees for 45 minutes.

Scoop ¼ cup squash and mash or blend with butter. Sweeten, adding fruit puree, and mix together.

(Use the remaining squash for adult meals, or cube squash and store in freezer.)

Makes 2 servings.

SPAGHETTI SQUASH

1 spaghetti squash
2 tablespoons spaghetti sauce or ¼ cup
   apricot/pineapple puree

Wash the squash. Cut it in half lengthwise and remove seeds. Bake, cut side down, in a pan with ½-inch of water at 350 degrees for 45 minutes. Turn the cut side up and bake until the squash is tender, between 30 and 40 minutes.

When you run a fork through the squash, it will release spaghetti-like strings. Blend to smooth consistency, ¼ cup squash and spaghetti sauce or fruit puree. (Store the remaining squash in freezer, or use in adult meal.)

Makes 1–3 servings.

Adult meal suggestion:
Serve squash with a topping of spaghetti sauce or mashed with butter.

BUTTERNUT SQUASH

1 butternut squash
1 teaspoon butter
Milk as needed for consistency
Sprinkle of nutmeg or cinnamon

Wash the squash and halve it lengthwise. Remove seeds. Bake with the cut side down in a baking dish at 350 degrees for about 50 minutes or until tender.

Blend ¼ cup squash for baby with butter, milk, and a sprinkle of nutmeg or cinnamon. Cut the balance of squash into pieces, and store in freezer or serve with a family meal.

Makes 1–2 servings.

ZUCCHINI SQUASH

1 zucchini squash
2 tablespoons tomato-based sauce
2 teaspoons Parmesan cheese
Drops of lemon juice

Thoroughly wash and do not peel zucchini squash. Cut in ¼-inch round slices. Steam, using a steam basket with a small amount of water for 4 to 6 minutes until tender. Except in soups, the flavor is more pleasing when cooked slightly crisp.

Blend with cooking juices and a few drops of lemon. For another flavor, add tomato-based sauce, such as spaghetti sauce, and blend together. Sprinkle with Parmesan cheese.

Makes 3–4 servings.

SWEETIE'S SWEET POTATO AND FRUIT

SWEET POTATO, BANANA, AND APPLE

2 medium-sized apples, skinned and thinly sliced
⅓ cup water
1 baked sweet potato, (see page 36)
1 banana, sliced
1 teaspoon butter
Dash of cinnamon

Cook sliced apples in water until tender.

Scoop sweet potato from skin, and discard skin.

Put all ingredients in blender, and puree. As the toddler can accept foods with small soft lumps, this recipe is excellent mashed, leaving a few lumps.

Makes 4–6 servings.

QUICK SWEET POTATO AND PINEAPPLE

1 baked sweet potato (see page 36)
¼ cup pineapple chunks

Scoop sweet potato from the shell.

In a blender, puree sweet potato and pineapple chunks with enough juice to make the appropriate consistency.

Makes 2–4 servings.

SWEET POTATO FINGER FOODS

2 large baked sweet potatoes
1 egg, beaten
2 tablespoons unbleached white flour
1 tablespoon milk
1 tablespoon melted butter
¼ teaspoon parsley, very finely chopped
½ cup bread crumbs
2 tablespoons cooking oil

Mix bread crumbs and parsley and set aside.

Scoop potato out of skin, and blend with all other ingredients, except bread crumb mixture and oil.

Heap the sweet potato mixture on a tablespoon and drop into the bread crumbs. Roll to form a small ball, and repeat with remaining sweet potato mixture.

Using a heavy skillet, heat oil on medium heat. Fry the balls, turning them on each side.

Fry for 2–3 minutes, or until the balls are golden brown. Place them carefully on paper towels to absorb the oil. They should be served warm, but check the temperature yourself before giving them to your baby.

If you wish to serve the remainder of these finger foods to the rest of your family, they can be maintained in an oven for a short time.

For adults these balls are great dipped in your favorite fresh salsa sauce.

Makes 14–18 balls.

IT'S SO YAM GOOD

YAMS AND MARSHMALLOWS

1 15-ounce can yams
¼ cup drained crushed pineapple (save juice)
½ cup minimarshmallows

Heat yams to a boil in saucepan; drain.

In blender, blend yams and pineapple, adding enough pineapple juice for appropriate consistency.

Spray a baking pan with nonstick agent. Spread the yam and pineapple mixture in the baking pan. Sprinkle marshmallows on top.

Broil until golden brown, about 2–4 minutes.

Makes 6–8 servings.

YAM 'N' HAM

1 15-ounce can yams
¼ cup drained pineapple chunks (save juice)
¼ cup cooked ham, finely minced

Bring yams, including juice, to a boil; drain.

Mix yams, pineapple chunks and ham in a blender, adding retained pineapple juice as needed for puree.

Options: Sliced bananas on top will add to the flavor and fun when the baby is developed enough for simple finger foods and a baby spoon.

Makes 8–10 servings.

I YAM WHAT I YAM

1 15-ounce can yams
6 green beans, steamed
Pineapple juice, as required for consistency

Puree yams and green beans in a blender using pineapple juice to sweeten and moisturize as desired. Serve and store additional servings in an ice cube tray. Freeze.

Makes 10 servings.

BEETS

Why are beets all by themselves? Because everything they touch turns red. Is that any reason to exclude them? Certainly not! Just be prepared to drape your baby from the tip of her nose to her pink baby toes. If she likes to blow bubbles, mom had better cover up, too.

PREPARING BEETS

2 small beets
1 squeeze lemon juice

Wash beets and cut off the tops, leaving about 1 inch. Cover beets with water in a saucepan and bring to a boil; cover pan with a lid.

Cook for about 50 minutes, and test with a fork for tenderness. When done, remove and drain. Cool beets with cold water, then peel and slice.

Puree with a few drops of lemon juice, adding water as needed for appropriate consistency.

Makes 2–3 servings.

BABY BEETS À L'ORANGE

2 small cooked beets
2 tablespoons cottage cheese
Orange juice as required for consistency

Make puree using beets and cottage cheese. Stir in orange juice to make a smooth consistency. At about ten months, if the baby is accepting soft lumps in his food, add the cottage cheese after making a puree using orange juice and beets.

Makes 2–4 servings.

Adults:
Present beets in julienne strips, slices for salads, as garnish, or hot and buttered with any meal.

BEETS AND CARROTS

Another great color spectacular! When your baby can eat small soft pieces of food with his fingers, this is a good food choice.

**2 small beets
1 medium-sized carrot**

Boil the beets until they are very tender, about 50 minutes. Peel and grate, or julienne the beets.

Coarsely grate carrot. Steam until soft, using a strainer to contain the small pieces of carrot, about 10 minutes.

Chill them separately, then mix together when serving.

If the baby still needs a puree, blend together, and add cooking juices as required for consistency.

Makes 3–4 servings.

Ideas for adults:

**½ cup julienned beets
¼ cup grated carrot
½ cup cooked peas
1 cucumber, paper thin slices**

Chill beets, carrots, peas, and cucumber in the refrigerator, keeping beets separate until just before serving. Mix together and serve with garlic, salad dressing.

Salad dressing:
¼ cup salad oil, 2 tablespoons lime juice, ½ clove minced garlic, and 1 teaspoon chopped parsley. Chill and refrigerate overnight before serving. Shake and serve.

MEATS, POULTRY, AND FISH

Small amounts of meats, poultry, and fish from the family meals will make many baby purees and meals. Quick single meals for your baby can be produced by stewing small portions of meat, chicken, or white fish.

Handling meats, poultry, and fish

- Check freshness. Discard foods that appear or smell aged.
- Thaw frozen meat, fish, or poultry in the refrigerator.
- To avoid bacteria, use separate cutting boards for:
  1. Meat
  2. Poultry
  3. Fish
- Thoroughly wash hands and all utensils that have come in contact with raw meats, poultry, or fish.
- Always make certain that meats, poultry, and fish are thoroughly cooked before serving.
- Never let stand at room temperature.

Making Baby Meals From Roasts
Roasts that work well for baby meals (and family meals) are as follows:

Pork	Pork blade roast
Beef	Beef chuck pot roast
Lamb	Lamb shoulder roast

Remove fat, gristle, and bone before preparing baby's meat. Cube the meat, and stew. Puree, adding fluids for texture.

First feedings will pour from the spoon. Gradually decrease the fluids as your child develops. The next stage is a soft texture that will drop from the spoon.

VEAL PUREE

1 pound boneless veal steak
Fluid, as needed for puree consistency (water, cooking juices, already tried fruit juices, or formula)

Using a meat mallet, pound a portion of boneless veal steak until steak is about ⅛-inch thick. Melt a small amount of margarine in a skillet. Cook the veal for about 2 minutes on each side until done. Cube veal steak, and place in blender. Add fluids, to make the appropriate consistency for your baby. Puree.

A one-pound steak will make 4 adult servings. Baby's early feedings will be very liquefied. Each adult serving will produce at least 3 baby servings when fluids are added. Freeze servings in covered ice cube trays and heat them each when you are serving.

Makes 12 baby servings.

CHICKEN PUREE

1 medium chicken breast (¾ pound)
Fluid, as needed for consistency (water, cooking juices,
    already tried fruit juices, or formula)

Skin chicken breast, then rinse under cold water. Place in
a heavy pan and add 1½ cups of water to cover. Bring
water to a boil. Cover pan with lid, reduce heat, and simmer
for 40 minutes. The chicken meat will be tender when done
and the coloration will no longer be pink.

Drain and retain cooking fluids. Cube chicken, and puree
with saved liquid or other suggested fluids.

*Storing: Pureed chicken must not sit at room tem-
            perature. Freeze, and store immediately
            after puree is made.

**Reheating: Poultry should be heated to about 185 de-
            grees. Puree will bubble when it reaches
            that temperature

When the baby's doctor approves spices, the chicken
may be flavored while cooking with herbs such as: basil,
sage, or thyme. When using these spices, place them in a
tea sieve to make them easier to remove from the chicken
broth.

Other flavorful additions can enhance the aroma and
taste: parsley, celery, carrots, green beans, and zucchini.
The first feedings, however, are *just chicken and fluid pureed.*

Strain and refrigerate the broth for use in another family
meal or to make a delicious soup.

One medium chicken breast will serve two adults. Depending on how much fluid you are adding for your baby's development, you will yield different amounts when you puree. In the first feedings, each adult serving will probably yield three baby servings. Which fluid you choose to use will also affect yield.

FISH PUREE

1 white fish fillet
Fluid as needed for consistency (water, vegetable cooking juices, apple juice, or chicken broth)

Poaching may be the quickest and easiest method to use in preparing fish for a single serving baby meal. We don't suggest storing fish after cooking.

    Bring chicken broth or other fluid to a boil in a saucepan. Place a 3-inch cut of the fillet (or all of it if the family is joining in), in a slotted spoon and carefully lower into chicken broth. Reduce the heat. Cover with a lid and simmer from 4 to 6 minutes for ½-inch thick fillet. Puree with liquids. First fish servings should pour from the spoon.

HAM PUREE

¼ cup cubed ham, precooked (fat removed)
Fluid, as needed for consistency (water, apple juice,
   pineapple juice, or formula)

Blend ham with pineapple juice or other fluid to make appropriate consistency for your baby. First feedings of ham
will pour from the spoon. Ham is often better accepted
when blended with vegetables or fruits. Puree vegetables
or fruits that the baby has already tried.
   Store in covered ice cube trays and freeze.
   The number of servings will depend on the amount of
fluids you use to puree. The first ham feedings will pour
and you should reap about 6 baby servings.

TURKEY PUREE

1 cup white turkey meat, prebaked and cubed
Fluid, as needed for consistency (apple or pear juice,
   water, or vegetable cooking juices)

Cube prebaked turkey, and add fluids. Although we use
ground turkey meat in various recipes for quick meals,
baked turkey is preferable in making purees to store in the
freezer.

Makes 8–10 servings.

CHICKEN, RICE, AND EVERYTHING NICE

¼ **cup cubed cooked chicken**
¼ **cup cooked white rice, soft**
½ **cup fruit puree**
Juice as needed for consistency

Juice and fruit options:

- Apricot or peach puree
- Cooked half peach
- Unsweetened pineapple
- Applesauce
- Apple juice
- Pear juice

Blend chicken with rice, and add fruit purees and preferred fluids for consistency and flavor.

Makes 8–10 servings
(Pouring consistency).

LITTLE PEOPLE'S CHICKEN POT PIE

The whole family can enjoy the baby's saucy chicken in pastry shells. For variety, try serving over biscuits instead of shells.

2½ to 3 pound chicken (broiler or fryer)
1 cup green peas (fresh or frozen)
1 carrot, thinly sliced
½ cup celery, chopped
1 onion, finely chopped
1 bay leaf
1 can mushroom soup
Milk, as required for consistency
1 dash soy sauce
1 package (6) frozen pastry shells (cooked according to package directions)

Separate parts of chicken; wash.

Cover chicken with water, about 3 quarts, in a dutch oven, or a large covered, oven-proof pot. Bring to a boil. Reduce heat, cover pan, and simmer for 25 minutes.

Skim chicken cooking juices, and add green peas, carrot, celery, and onion to the chicken.

Break bay leaf into pieces and place it in a tea sieve; place sieve in cooking water.

Simmer for 12–15 minutes until vegetables are tender and chicken has lost pink color.

Remove chicken from pot; skin, cool, and cube. Drain vegetables, storing broth.

Combine mushroom soup and sufficient milk to make a

creamy texture in dutch oven. Add a few drops of soy sauce, for color and flavor. Stir.

Stir in vegetables and cubed chicken (tea sieve removed). Cook until sauce is bubbly. Serve in cooked pastry shells for babies who can chew soft foods. Blend to puree when serving younger babies.

Adults and older children:
Garnish with fine strips of red bell pepper, and a sprinkle of paprika.

Makes 2 baby servings and 5 adult servings.

HAM AND RICE, OH ISN'T IT NICE?

½ cup precooked ham, cubed (make sure you cut off all fat)
4 ounces cooked rice, soft
Pineapple juice as needed for consistency

Puree in blender, warm, and serve.
Store excess in freezer.

Makes 8–10 servings.

IT'S A VEAL GOOD DINNER WITH RICE

¼ pound boneless veal steak
2 tablespoons butter or margarine
½ cup soft cooked rice

Pound veal steak with a mallet until it is about ⅛-inch thick.

Cook in a skillet with butter or margarine for 2 minutes on each side, saving the cooked veal drippings. Cube the veal steak and place in a blender. Add rice to the blender.

Stir water into the skillet to make a tasty fluid for use in blending. Pour this into blender, using the appropriate amount for the consistency your baby requires. Store extra servings in the freezer.

Makes 6–8 servings.

TEMPTING TURKEY AND RICE

½ cup cooked turkey meat, cubed
½ cup cooked rice, soft
Vegetable cooking juices, or chicken broth as needed
   for appropriate consistency

Add all ingredients to blender. Puree, adding fluids as needed for the baby's preferred consistency. Extra servings may be frozen.

Makes 6–8 servings.

FABULOUS FISH

Selecting quality fish

Nothing is more important than selecting good raw ingredients in preparation for excellent meals. Freshness of fish is of primary importance. Top quality frozen is fine, also, if the freezing has been maintained and the packaging appears to be in good condition. When buying fresh fish, there are three main tests for determining freshness:

* ODOR
* APPEARANCE
* TOUCH

The odor test is easily accomplished. Fish should have a mild aroma. If it has a strong fishy odor, it is probably not fresh and should be avoided.

Appearance is important. Whole fish will have shiny skin, red or pink gills, and clear eyes. If you are buying fillets or steaks, look for a moist appearance—not flaky texture—and a clean cut without discoloration.

Touching the fish is another way to determine quality. There should be an elasticity and firmness to the fillet. If you press a finger to a whole fish, it then should spring back slightly.

Storing, handling, and thawing fish

Fish should be prepared as soon as possible after you purchase it, preferably the same day. When you cannot do that, you may store it in the refrigerator for a day or two— no more. For best storage, loosely wrap the fish in clear plastic wrap. Place frozen fish in your freezer as soon as possible. Thawing and refreezing is not acceptable. Do not thaw fish outside of the refrigerator. It will not thaw evenly, and the outside areas are apt to spoil. Six hours in the refrigerator should do the trick for almost any fillet or steak.

One half hour in salted water, or water with a splash of vinegar, will decrease any fishy taste. Rinse all fish thoroughly before cooking.

Remember these rules for safe fish preparation:

• Thaw fish in refrigerator
• Do not thaw in water or at room temperature
• Never refreeze fish

Methods of preparing fish include: poaching, baking, broiling, and frying. Fish is a great alternative to meats and poultry. It offers an excellent source of protein and other nutrients.

Increasingly, fish are being raised in fish farms. The source of water where the fish are growing is very important. Farms offer an opportunity for fish to grow to adulthood in a pollution-free water environment. Your local farmer's market will most likely be the best place to find this type of fish.

Anytime you have handled fish you must wash your hands thoroughly with soap and water. All containers, cutting surfaces, and implements must also be washed with care when they have been in contact with fish. Wooden cutting boards should not be used with fish, poultry, or raw meats. Their absorbency allows bacteria to grow, and can cause illness when other foods are eaten that have been in contact with the wooden surface.

FISH BONES MAY BE SMALL OR FINE. USE CAUTION AND BE SURE THAT ALL BONES HAVE BEEN REMOVED BEFORE FEEDING FISH TO YOUR BABY.

MOUTH-OPENING FISH

Fillets of Orange Roughy, Perch, or Sole

Fillets are supposed to be boneless but always check for fine, uneasily detected bones, and remove them.

Orange roughy, perch, or sole fillets can be baked, broiled, or poached. When you are preparing fish for the family meal, you may need to remove the seasonings from the baby's portion before blending, assuming that seasonings are not yet acceptable. We started feeding our babies seasonings such as herbs, onions, and natural flavorings at a very early age. Opinions on the subject of flavorings vary, and it is up to you and your doctor to decide about including them.

POACHED FILLETS

½-inch thick fish fillet
1 cup water, chicken broth, or vegetable cooking
  juices

The quickest method of preparing a single serving of fish fillet for your baby is poaching. Fluid for poaching may be chicken broth, vegetable cooking juices, or water.

Cut off a single portion of fish fillet (about 3 inches), and gently place it in a saucepan with 1 cup of boiling water, chicken broth, or vegetable cooking juices. (We like to use a slotted spoon to place the fish in the fluid.) When the fluid returns to boiling, cover the pan and lower the heat. Simmer for 6 minutes. The fish will be flaky when done.

Older babies can eat this tender fish when simply mashed. Younger fish lovers will appreciate blending with a modest amount of fish stock, or water.

2 or 3 drops of lemon juice will enhance the flavor.

Serve and do not store.

Serve the remainder of fish fillet in a family meal, either poached, or cooked in another manner.

Makes 1 serving.

BABY FRANK'S FISH & BROCCOLI

1 ½-inch thick fillet of sole or flounder
1 cup chicken broth
3 steamed broccoli flowerets
1 tablespoon baby rice cereal
Milk as needed for consistency

Rinse fish fillet and pat dry.

Bring chicken broth to a boil in a flat-bottomed pan, with room for a wire basket insert.

Gently place the fillet on the bottom of a strainer. Insert the strainer in pan, and bring to a boil once again. Reduce heat and simmer, covering the pan with a lid.

Simmer for 6 minutes. Fish will be flaky when done.

Remove the basket and drain.

Place ⅓ of the fillet in a blender with 1 broccoli floweret. Then blend, adding baby rice cereal and milk as needed for appropriate texture.

Serve the balance of the fillet and broccoli for one family meal.

Makes 1 serving.

Adult dinner:
Use remainder of fillet for adult dinner or increase the quantity to meet your family's needs.

Place cooked fillets on a plate and cover with heated mushroom sauce (recipe to follow.)

Make a line of pureed broccoli or pureed spinach down the center of each fillet. Serve with rice pilaf and broccoli.

Place a garnish of radishes, cherry tomatoes, parsley and a slice of lemon on each plate.

MUSHROOM SAUCE

1 can mushroom soup
½ cup milk
1 dash of soy sauce, generous
1 sprinkle of garlic salt

Mix and heat before serving.

HAL'S HALIBUT

1 1-inch thick halibut steak
2 tablespoons butter or margarine, melted
1 squeeze lemon juice
¼ cup green vegetable puree
¼ cup mashed potatoes

Rinse the halibut steak and pat it dry.
Brush the steak with melted butter or margarine. Salt and pepper to taste.
　　Place on broiler pan, four inches below heat.
　　Broil for 5 minutes, turn, and brush top with butter. Continue under broiler for 6 or 7 more minutes and use a fork to test. When it is done it will flake on the fork easily.
　　Cut a 1-inch square of halibut steak, remove all bones, and puree (or mash for older toddlers who are accepting soft foods with some texture). A few drops of lemon juice will heighten the flavor. Serve with a green vegetable puree and mashed potatoes.

Makes one complete meal.

For Adults:
Serve the remainder of halibut with asparagus spears, mashed potatoes, lemon wedges.

BAKING HALIBUT

This recipe will be served as the baby is approaching his first birthday. Onions are introduced sparingly. Be watchful for the baby's reaction. If there is any discomfort or fussiness, leave the onions out and try them again later.

1 1-inch thick halibut steak
4 tablespoons orange juice
1 tablespoon lemon juice
1 tablespoon parsley, finely chopped
1 green onion, finely chopped
1 tablespoon melted butter

Mix all ingredients except the fish in a small bowl.

Place the halibut steak in a lidded baking pan. Spread the mixture over the halibut, and cover with lid.

Bake at 400 degrees for about 20 minutes. Fish will flake easily when done.

Remove bones, and puree, or mash as required for baby's development. It may be necessary to add water for appropriate consistency,

Makes 1 baby serving and two adult servings.

ELISE'S ELEGANT FISH AND VEGETABLES

2 white fish fillets
2 cups chicken broth
4 large mushrooms
1 garlic clove
2 tablespoons butter
1 zucchini
1 summer squash
1 carrot
Orange juice as required for consistency

Rinse white fish, and pat dry. Poach in chicken broth; remove fish from broth, and save.

Sauté sliced mushrooms and minced garlic in butter.

Thinly slice zucchini and summer squash, and coarsely grate the carrot. Then lightly steam these vegetables.

Add the steamed vegetables to the sautéd mixture, and toss.

When the baby is still requiring pureed foods, blend all vegetables and fish together. Orange juice may be added for flavor and more moisture. Prepare about 3 inches of fillet (½-inch thick) and ¼ cup mixed vegetables for the baby's dinner. The remaining fish and vegetables will make a wonderful family dinner. Adults will enjoy this fish with the vegetables spooned on top.

PASTAS

Types of Pastas for Baby

- Alphabets
- Tiny bow ties
- Thin spaghetti
- Baby rings
- Small shells
- Small egg noodles

Precooked pasta for easy, quick meals

After cooking pasta according to the package instructions, place pasta in a colander; drain, and rinse. Turn the pasta into a moisture proof and vapor proof container with a lid. Freeze. Should you desire to freeze the pasta in individual portions, freeze in 4-ounce containers. Pasta may be frozen for a month or more.

Some mothers prefer to remove frozen pasta from the containers and store individual servings in zip-lock bags. This saves your freezer dishes for other items.

When serving the pasta, bring 2 cups water to boiling in a saucepan. Place the frozen pasta in boiling water and return to boil. Cook for 1 minute, or as required for softness. Drain.

Cut longer forms of pasta into short pieces for toddler meals. Smaller infant's dinner will need to be blended.

PASTA PLEASERS

Pasta pleasers are enticing baby meals that can be enjoyed by adults also. Baby's dinner can be separated from the adults and blended or mashed depending on the texture required for your baby. Save the seasonings for the adult portion, until your baby is at least one year old.

BABY FETTUCCINE—FOR MOMS AND DADS, TOO

1 4-ounce package fettuccine
1 tablespoon butter
¼ cup Parmesan cheese
3 tablespoons light cream, room temperature

Cook fettuccine using package instructions.

Melt butter in saucepan, and add the drained fettuccine. Stir, and cook over low heat.

Add Parmesan cheese and cream. Quickly toss the fettuccine until a coating covers all the pasta.

Measure ⅓ cup of mixture, and puree in a blender or grinder. As the baby develops, at about ten months, the pasta can be minced or mashed with a fork.

Pureed spinach, meat, chicken, or fish will add flavor and nutrition to this meal.

The extra baby serving can be stored in the refrigerator for one day.

After removing one or two four-ounce baby servings, there will remain three adult portions for a family meal.

Adult version:
Lightly season pasta with nutmeg.

VERMICELLI AND LIVER

4-ounce package vermicelli
2 carrots
2 small white potatoes
6 asparagus spears
6 chicken livers
4 mushroom caps
Milk as required for consistency

Cook vermicelli according to package instructions.
Steam carrots, potatoes, and asparagus, for 20 minutes.
Sauté chicken livers and mushrooms in butter until livers
are no longer pink.

For Babies:
Puree 1 liver, ½ carrot, ½ potato, and 1 asparagus spear
adding milk, as required, to make a creamy texture. If the
baby has developed sufficiently to accept soft, grain-like
texture, mash ¼ cup vermicelli with fork and mix it into
the puree. Pasta may be pureed for less developed babies
(under 10 months).

Makes 2 baby servings and 3 adult servings.

For Adults:
Cube or cut vegetables and livers into bite-sized pieces.
Then mix vegetables, except asparagus, with basic white
sauce. Add chicken livers and mix.

Spoon over vermicelli and top with a spear of asparagus.
A dash of paprika will add color and zest!
(*Basic White Sauce:* page 130)

ORIENTAL RAMEN NOODLES AND VEGETABLES

¼ cup carrots, julienned
¼ cup spinach, finely chopped
1 green onion, cut in 1-inch pieces
¼ cup fresh peas, shelled
½ cup cooked beef, cubed
2 packages Ramen noodles
Pineapple juice as needed for consistency

Steam vegetables (see steam time chart page 104), using a strainer over water in a covered pan. You will add the spinach in the last 6 minutes of steaming. Following the steam chart, remove adult's vegetables and continue steaming the baby's vegetables for another 2 minutes, or until very soft.

Cook Ramen noodles, leaving the seasoning (packet) out of the pot. Puree ½ cup of the following: carrots, spinach, peas, cubed beef, and ramen noodles. Add pineapple juice as needed for consistency.

Makes 1–2 servings
(for babies over 10 months).

Adult version:
Add Ramen seasoning (in packet) to pot. Place ramen, vegetables, and meat in serving bowls and top with broth.

Ramen is a quick answer for meals in a hurry. You can make many fast meals using leftovers. Most of the Ramen mixes do not contain eggs. Check the ingredients if you need an egg-free pasta for your baby.

PASTA RECIPES JUST FOR BABY

EGG NOODLES, CHEESE, AND VEAL

4 ounces veal, cubed
1 small sprig of parsley, chopped
1 pinch fresh rosemary
4 ounces egg noodles, cooked
1 tablespoon Parmesan cheese, grated
Milk, as required for consistency

Place parsley and rosemary in a tea sieve. Add veal and the tea sieve to sauce pan of boiling water. Reduce the heat to a slow simmer, and cook for ½ hour, or until tender.

Remove the tea sieve. Place egg noodles and veal in a blender. Add Parmesan cheese and milk as required for puree texture. Blend and serve.

(For most babies around ten months to a year, this food can be minced and mashed.)

Makes 2–4 servings.

NOODLING AROUND WITH VEAL AND VEGETABLES

1 zucchini, cut in moderately thin slices
1 slice onion, chopped
2 ½-inch strips of red bell pepper
4 ounces cooked veal or beef, cubed
4 ounces egg noodles, precooked

Steam all vegetables together for 10–12 minutes.

Heat precooked egg noodles in boiling water, and drain.

Blend and puree veal, vegetables, and noodles. Add vegetable cooking juices as needed for additional liquid. Serve or store in freezer.

Makes 6–8 servings.

BABY'S USING HIS NOODLE AND TURKEY TOO!

1 carrot, coarsely grated
1 finely chopped stalk of celery
2 medium-sized tomatoes, diced, skinned, and seeded
¼ small onion, chopped
3 tablespoons butter
1 small sprig parsley, chopped
1 pinch oregano
4 ounces cooked turkey meat
4 ounces noodles or spaghetti, precooked and cut in ¼-inch pieces

Sauté carrot, celery, tomatoes and brown onion for 4 minutes in a small skillet with half the butter.

Add enough water to cover the vegetables in skillet, stir. Enclose parsley and oregano in a tea sieve. Place the tea sieve in cooking water; simmer for 20 minutes.

Remove the sieve, and drain the vegetables, saving the cooking juices.

Melt remaining butter in the skillet, adding drained vegetables, minced turkey, and spaghetti.

As your baby approaches the one year mark, he may be able to eat this food after it's mashed with a fork. Until that time, make puree in a blender. Serve or store in freezer.

Makes 8–10 servings.

ALPHABET? WHAT'S THAT?

½ cup alphabet pasta
½ cup steamed asparagus
Milk as required for appropriate consistency

Cook alphabet pasta until it is so soft that it barely holds together.

Make a puree, blending steamed asparagus and milk.

Gently stir the pasta into the creamed asparagus, and serve.

Freeze remaining servings.

Makes 4 servings.

PASTA, BROCCOLI, MEAT, AND APRICOT

4 ounces fettucini, precooked
1 tablespoon butter
⅓ cup meat, minced or pureed
¼ cup vegetable puree
2 tablespoons apricot puree

Finely chop pasta and heat it in a skillet with butter. Stir in pureed meat, pureed vegetables, and pureed apricot. Pastas must be pureed until the baby is ready for granular texture. Check with your baby's doctor to find out best time for your baby. Serve or freeze to store. Do not refreeze foods.

Makes 3–4 servings.

RICE

Preparing rice for quick meals

Cook rice according to package instructions. Drain and rinse in colander. Freeze in 4-ounce moisture and vapor proof containers. Rice may be transferred to zip lock bags once frozen.

Heating precooked and frozen rice

When you are serving precooked frozen rice, place one 4-ounce serving with 1 tablespoon of water in a pan, and cover with a lid. Cook slowly for 1 minute. Test for softness, adding another tablespoon of water, and cooking for an additional minute if necessary. When freezing the rice, storing in a flat configuration, like a meat patty, will allow quicker reheating.

Rice combinations

- Rice cooked in chicken broth, or vegetable cooking juices
- Rice as a base for mixed dinners
- Rice in combination with fruits, puddings, and yogurts as desserts

DESSERTS

Good nutrition and the avoidance of rich foods and refined sugars is a family matter, not just a baby issue. Limiting these foods, while finding other ways to present "sweets," will definitely result in children who are more attentive in school, have stronger bodies, and are generally happier people. At a young age, children begin to desire foods that they see mom and dad eat. Through the years we have seen parents take a bite of the food that they want their baby to like. It works. Parents must see the importance of looking at their own diets to encourage children to desire good, nourishing foods.

Babies from six to twelve months do enjoy sweets. It is wise to serve sweet fruit purees as the last food of the meal to achieve a balanced diet. Reserving sweet tastes for last will encourage eating vegetables, meats, and the basics.

Fruits that are properly ripened will be enjoyed and do not require sweetening with sugar, honey, or sugar substitutes. If you are using canned fruits, rinse the syrup off of the fruit under cool water before serving. Many syrups are laden with sugars or sugar substitutes.

4

Third Step:
Foods For 12–18
Months

When your baby is one year old, he may have been introduced to as many as thirty-five foods. Using the rule of one new food each week, he should have explored many of the foods that the family eats regularly.

During the time from twelve months to eighteen months many things are changing in the baby's life. Most likely he will begin to stand up and walk on his own, push himself in a baby auto, dance to music, and explore rhythm. Also, during this time, you will see changes in the way the baby eats. He will want a small plastic glass to hold, and drink without mom's assistance. Many times he will use a fat bowled spoon with a short handle, or pick up food with his fingers.

Babies are wonderful mimics at this age. They will copy your mannerisms; how you move your hands, how you move your head, and almost anything that they see you do repetitively. Although most toddlers aren't using words, the "babble" will often have your voice inflections. Whatever you are eating will look appealing to your baby. This is the time to convert your baby to the foods that your family regularly eats. With your doctors approval, citrus fruits and some berries can be introduced. Aside from exotic foods, which most children do not enjoy, your baby will be eating minced or ground versions of family foods by his eighteenth month. Never force or pressure him to eat foods that he turns down. Making mealtime relaxed and happy is the best recipe for a happy, healthy baby.

Let's eat!

BREAKFASTS

BIG BATCH BASIC PANCAKE MIX

Make a large batch of pancake mix and store it in an airtight container so that preparing breakfast is fast. There are many uses for the mix.

Preparation:
10 cups all-purpose flour
⅓ cup baking powder
1 teaspoon salt
¼ cup white sugar
2 cups shortening

Mix all ingredients except shortening in a bowl. Be sure that the dry ingredients are thoroughly blended together.

Add the shortening to the dry mix. Cut the shortening into the dry mix until the mixture is the texture of coarse crumbs.

Place the mixture in an airtight and moisture proof freezer container. Store the mixture for up to 3 months in your freezer, using portions as needed in food preparation.

PEEK-A-BOO PANCAKES
WITH BANANAS

**1 cup Big Batch Basic Pancake Mix (see page 95 for
  recipe)**
1 egg, beaten
¾ cup milk
1 banana, sliced in rounds

Place pancake mix in a mixing bowl.

Add milk and eggs at once, and stir until blended.

Place banana slices in mixture, and stir.

Spoon 1 tablespoon of batter (to make dollar-sized pancakes), on a lightly greased skillet. Make sure that each pancake has at least one banana slice.

When pancakes have air bubbles and appear to be drying, it is time to turn them. When they are done, they will be a beautiful golden brown color.

Makes 12–14 dollar-sized pancakes.

Serving suggestions:
1. Top pancakes with a mixture of natural yogurt and mashed bananas.
2. Sprinkle powdered sugar on pancakes.

PANSY'S FAVORITE APPLE PANCAKES

1 cup Big Batch Basic Pancake Mix
1 egg, beaten
¾ cup milk
1 apple, grated

Prepare Pansy's Favorite Apple Pancakes as you prepared Peek-a-Boo Banana Pancakes (on page 96), substituting the grated apples for bananas.

Topping:
¼ cup powdered sugar
Pinch of finely grated lemon peel
1 teaspoon cinnamon

Mix all ingredients and sprinkle on Pansy's Favorite Apple Pancakes.

Makes 18–20 pancakes for baby and family.

WHOLE WHEAT PANCAKES

A Toddler and Family Meal

2 cups whole wheat flour
½ cup wheat germ
2 teaspoons baking powder
1 teaspoon salt
1 tablespoon brown sugar
2 eggs
2½ cups milk
2 tablespoons cooking oil

Mix all dry ingredients together.

In a separate bowl, slightly beat eggs. Add milk and cooking oil. Stir.

Combine the egg and milk mixture with dry ingredients, and mix.

Lightly grease a skillet; heat. Spoon pancake mix onto the hot surface and watch each until bubbles appear and they begin to dry. Turn and finish cooking.

Serve with raspberry fruit puree and a touch of whipped cream. Baby's pancakes should be cut in finger food sized pieces.

This makes a great breakfast for the family and the toddler when he can chew soft foods.

Makes 20 pancakes.

Whipped Cream Suggestions:
It is easy to make fresh whipped cream and it tastes so much better than the prewhipped varieties. Just pour a little

heavy whipping cream into your wand blender, container, or small blender, and turn it on. Whip briefly, being watchful for the change in consistency. Stop immediately when the cream can form peaks. Add a few drops of vanilla when whipping. It is heavenly.

RAISIN' MY BABY WITH LOVE-ROLLED CREPES

1 cup all purpose flour
2 eggs
1 tablespoon vegetable cooking oil
1½ cups milk
¼ teaspoon salt

Mix all ingredients in a blender or by hand.

Lightly grease and heat a small skillet (6 inches), then remove it from heat.

Immediately place 2 tablespoons of crepe batter in the center of the hot skillet.

To spread the batter all over the bottom of the skillet, hold the skillet by its handle and tilt in all directions.

Return the skillet to heat and cook until the bottom side of the crepe is a golden color.

Turn the skillet upside down, allowing the crepe to settle on a paper towel.

Continue this process until all of the crepes have been cooked.

Makes 16–18 servings.

RAISIN CREPE FILLING

¼ cup raisin molé (recipe on page 146)
½ cup applesauce
Dash of cinnamon

Mix raisin molé with applesauce and add a dash of cinnamon. Stir, warm, and then and fill the center line of crepes with mixture. Roll crepes and serve.

Excess sugar is not recommended, but if you choose you may sprinkle the finished crepes with a dusting of powdered sugar.

STRAWBERRY CREPES

1 cup fresh strawberries, crushed
¼ cup powdered sugar
1 teaspoon cinnamon

Prepare crepes as above, fill each with crushed strawberries, and roll. Sprinkle with powdered sugar, and a dash of cinnamon. Serve.

THE WHOLE EGG: SCRAMBLED AND FLUFFY

1 egg (don't forget to wash the shell)
1 teaspoon milk (if allergic to milk, use water)
1 teaspoon butter

Break the egg into a small bowl. Add milk or water, and beat with a fork.

Slowly melt a rounded teaspoon of butter in a small skillet or sauté pan, add the egg, and cook over low heat.

Stir gently until the egg is no longer runny. Remove from pan and serve. May be served with strips of dry toast for a simple breakfast.

Makes 1 serving.

FRENCH TOAST

1 egg
1 pinch salt
¼ cup milk
2 slices bread
2 tablespoons sweet fruit puree or Strawberry Sauce
  (see page 132)
1 teaspoon powdered sugar
½ teaspoon butter

Beat egg slightly; add salt, milk, and stir. Cut bread into four strips. Dip the bread on both sides into the egg mixture. Cook on reasonably high heat in a greased frying pan. Turn so both sides are golden brown. Serve with fruit puree or Strawberry Sauce.

Makes 2 servings.

SOMETHING NICE AND PRUNE WHIP

2 stewed prunes
¼ cup vanilla yogurt
1 pancake or 1 slice French toast

Puree prunes (pressed through colander), then add yogurt.
Mix until smooth.
   Spread on pancakes or french toast.

Makes 1 serving.

EGG PANCAKE

1 egg
2 teaspoons milk

Lightly beat egg and stir in milk.
   Pour egg into a heated and lightly greased small skillet.
Roll the pan to spread egg over the entire surface. Cook
over medium heat turning once.
   Serve with orange sauce (recipe page 103), and a sprinkle
of powdered sugar.

Makes 1 serving.

ORANGE SAUCE

4 segments navel orange
2 tablespoons butter
2 tablespoons whole wheat flour
1 cup orange juice

Remove the membranes from orange segments and break orange into very small pieces.

Melt butter and add flour, stirring and cooking over medium heat for two minutes.

Add orange juice, while continuously stirring. Simmer and stir until it is a creamy and thickened sauce.

Just before serving, add the pieces of orange. Serve warm.

Makes 4 servings.

VEGETABLES

Most of the time, your baby will probably eat vegetables prepared individually. The wonderful fresh flavors will be appreciated while spices, mixed vegetables, and fancy combinations really aren't necessary.

As you integrate the family's eating preferences with baby meals, you can gradually work towards the day when you will all eat the same foods. There are recipes and combinations in this chapter that will work well for baby and family. For your convenience and for the occasions when you will prepare vegetables separately, we are charting the

time required for steaming most of the vegetables you may
choose to serve your little one.

Vegetables are not boring!

VEGETABLE	TIME REQUIRED FOR STEAMING	
Asparagus	4–8	Minutes
Green beans	18–22	Minutes
Beets	40–50	Minutes (boil)
Broccoli	8–12	Minutes
Brussels sprouts	10–15	Minutes
Cabbage	10–12	Minutes
Carrots	8–10	Minutes
Cauliflower	8–12	Minutes
Celery	7–10	Minutes
Parsnips	8–10	Minutes
Green peas	12–15	Minutes
White potatoes	20	Minutes
Sweet potatoes	30–35	Minutes (boil)
Spinach	3–5	Minutes
Turnips	10–15	Minutes
Zucchini	4–6	Minutes

STEAMED MIXED VEGETABLES

For toddlers who can chew soft vegetables and for their
favorite moms and dads

The steamed vegetable platter toppings:

Whether you serve the baby from the family vegetable
platter or blend the foods, flavorful toppings will be appreciated. With the exception of corn, which should not be
served until age two, most vegetables are acceptable. Try

them one at a time, and in small quantities. All foods must be approved by the baby's doctor.

- Hot cauliflower topped with grated cheddar cheese
- Drops of soy sauce over broccoli
- A squeeze of lemon juice on green beans
- Cooked green pepper and onions in blended purees
- Butter on corn (for parents only)

Salt and pepper are not necessary when natural flavorings are used in combination with the melding of the vegetable flavors. The vegetable platter is so delightfully colorful that it can be the centerpiece for sumptuous meals with guests.

SPINACH PUREE

1 bunch spinach
1 squeeze lemon

Spinach must be cleaned carefully. Submerge it in salted water and agitate. Next, rinse each leaf individually. Drain, and remove stems. The work is definitely worthwhile!

Steam spinach for 5 minutes.

Drain, and puree spinach in a blender, adding cooking juices as required for texture; add a few drops of lemon for flavor.

Serve baby his portion, and do not store. Use balance for an adult meal.

Makes 1 baby serving and 2 adult servings.

MASHED POTATOES AND SPINACH

Prepare this recipe when serving spinach for an adult dinner. Make spinach puree recipe on page 105.

1 medium white potato
½ cup spinach puree
milk, as needed for consistency
1 teaspoon Parmesan cheese

Wash, peel, and cube potato. Steam for about 20 minutes,
until tender.
    Blend potato and spinach puree, adding milk as needed.
Grated Parmesan cheese will add a zesty flavor. Store in
cubes, frozen.

Makes 4 servings.

LATER ON WHEN CHEESE
IS FINE, ASPARAGUS

By now, our baby gourmet probably loves asparagus or at
least tolerates it. Remember to prepare asparagus so that
there are no strings. To make this vegetable more interesting for babies and adults, we offer some flavorful combinations to be shared.

6 asparagus spears (select thin, young spears)
2 tablespoons cheddar cheese, grated
Vegetable cooking juices or milk, as required for
**   consistency**

Clean asparagus in salt water and rinse thoroughly. Remove the woody ends, snapping them off where they break easily.

Use the steam chart for steaming preparation on page 104. If you chose to boil the spears, cook with a lidded pan in boiling water for 2–4 minutes, depending on the size of the spears. Test for tenderness with a fork.

Drain asparagus, saving the cooking juices.

While the asparagus is hot enough to melt cheese, cover the spears with grated cheese, and allow to melt.

Blend to puree, adding cooking juices or milk for consistency. Serve, storing excess in freezer.

Makes 3 servings.

Finger foods:
When the baby is enjoying finger foods, asparagus spears cooked until very tender will be excellent with a dip or salad dressing. This can be a great between-meal snack.

REMEMBER THE HAM AND ASPARAGUS

¼ cup cooked ham, cubed
½ cup cooked asparagus, with melted cheddar cheese
Unsweetened pineapple juice, as needed for
   consistency

Blend all ingredients in blender, adding juice to make appropriate consistency.

Makes 6–8 servings.

STUFFED SQUASH
(Butternut or Acorn Varieties)

Preparing the Squash
Set the oven at 350 degrees.

Thoroughly wash the outside of the squash, and cut in half. Remove the seeds and stringy pulp.

Place upside down in a baking pan, and bake for 30 minutes.

Turn the squash halves so that the cut side is up, and stuff squash centers with bread stuffing mix.

Bake covered with foil for 20 more minutes.

Bread Stuffing:

¼ **cup onion, finely chopped**
1 **apple, grated**
1 **cup seasoned bread stuffing mix**
4 **tablespoons water or apple juice**

Sauté onions, and mix well with all other ingredients in a bowl.

To Serve:
Squash may be mashed with a fork and a bit of butter. For a finer puree, it can be blended with milk or apple juice.

A puree can be blended using the stuffing, squash, and apple juice.

Near eighteen months many babies will enjoy sucking and chewing on very soft cubes of squash with a bit of butter on top.

CASSANDRA'S GREEN BEANS AND COTTAGE CHEESE

6 fresh green beans
6 tablespoons cottage cheese

Wash beans thoroughly. Remove ends, pulling strings off in the process; then cut beans. Cook in a small pan with a lid, using sufficient boiling water to cover. Cook for 25 minutes. Check with fork for tenderness. Drain, reserving cooking juices.

Puree beans and cottage cheese in a blender. In the latter months of this time period, some children will enjoy having the beans mashed with a fork and simply stirred into cottage cheese.

Makes 3–4 servings.

Adult version:
When serving adults, increase bean recipe. Wash and seed a large tomato. Stuff it with the bean/cottage cheese puree. Garnish with chopped chives, and a dash of paprika.

STUFFED POTATOES

Presenting foods in a creative way encourages children to explore different foods and makes mealtime more exciting. Stuffed potatoes are a special way for babies to enjoy mashed potatoes and other potato mixtures.

BASIC STUFFED POTATOES

1 large baked potato
1 tablespoon butter
Milk, as needed for consistency
1 tablespoon cheddar cheese, grated (optional)

Cut a baked potato in half lengthwise and scoop out the pulp, saving the skins.

Mash the potato, adding butter, and then milk as needed, to make the appropriate consistency.

Replace the mashed potato in the skins.

Bake for additional 20 minutes in a preheated 375 degree oven.

Cheese Variety:
Sprinkle grated cheddar cheese on top of each potato half before baking.

Makes 4 servings.

TUNA POTATO BOAT

2 baked white potatoes
2 tablespoons butter
Milk as needed for consistency
1 3½ ounce can white tuna, drained
½ cup steamed vegetables, chopped (Try using this
    combination: celery, carrots, onion and broccoli)
⅓ cup grated cheddar cheese

Cut potatoes in halves lengthwise, and scoop out the pulp, saving the skins. Mash the potato pulp, adding first butter, and then milk, as needed, for smooth and somewhat stiff texture.

Blend the tuna and vegetables.

Mix tuna/vegetable combination with mashed potato, and stuff the mixture into potato skins.

Generously sprinkle grated cheese on top.

Bake on a baking sheet in a preheated 375 degree oven for 20 minutes.

Makes 2 baby and 3 adult servings.

VEGETABLES AND TURKEY POTATOES

Prepare as with Tuna Potato Boat, substituting diced turkey meat for tuna. Sautéd mushrooms are a nice addition to this combination.

IT'S OKRA DOKRA WITH ME!

Okra is great in soups or mixed with other vegetables. Slice the okra and cook with other mixed vegetables. To cook, simmer for 30 minutes after water has been brought to a boil.

Good combinations with okra are: tomatoes, red bell peppers, green beans, carrots, peas, and potatoes.

SHE PICKED PARSNIPS FROM THE PARSNIP PATCH

1 cup parsnips, peeled and cut in ¼-inch slices
2 teaspoons parsley, finely chopped
1 tablespoon butter or margarine
2 tablespoons Swiss, cheddar, or Parmesan cheese
Milk (optional)

Cook sliced parsnips in a large skillet with butter or margarine. Cook for 8 to 9 minutes, turning frequently.

When parsnips are done, they will be tender. Drain excess butter and stir in parsley. While parsnips are steaming hot, sprinkle grated cheese on top and cover the serving bowl. When cheese is melted, serve.

Puree ¼ cup parsnips for your baby, adding milk for a creamier consistency, if required. Serve the remainder to your favorite adults.

Makes 1 baby and 2 adult servings.

BORED WITH PEAS?

½ cup fresh or frozen green peas
¼ cup Basic White Sauce (see page 130)
2 tablespoons Swiss cheese, grated
½ teaspoon chopped parsley

Cook peas, steaming fresh peas for 12–15 minutes, or following package instructions for frozen. Drain, saving cooking juices. Add to heated basic white sauce. While hot, stir in cheese and parsley. Mash or blend and serve, adding cooking juices if required for baby's preferred consistency. Serve.

Chopped chives may be substituted for parsley. When using either parsley or chives, add sparingly.

Makes 2–3 servings (or 1 baby and 1 adult serving).

SAUCY BEEF SPINACH

1 10-ounce package of frozen chopped spinach
¼ cup Saucy Beef Gravy (see page 131)

Cook frozen spinach according to package instructions, and drain. Add Saucy Beef Gravy; puree and serve. Do not store. Serve your baby and make the remainder part of an adult meal.

Makes 1 baby serving and 3 adult servings.

MEATS, POULTRY, AND FISH

DISH LICK'N LIVER & VEGETABLES

1 tablespoon butter
½ pound chicken livers, chopped
½ pound brown onion, finely chopped
1 large carrot, cut in thin slices
6 green beans
1 medium potato

Melt butter in skillet. Add chicken livers and onions. Stir and turn continuously over medium heat for 5 minutes, or until liver is no longer pink.

Steam green beans and potato for 10 minutes; add carrots and continue steaming about 10 more minutes. Test with a fork; when vegetables are soft, drain, saving the cooking fluid.

Blend liver and vegetables in blender, adding vegetable cooking fluids as needed for appropriate consistency.
Serve or freeze for later use.

Texture:
Texture should increase gradually as your baby can accept soft lumps and vegetables cut in small soft pieces. For this recipe, you could continue to puree the liver and onions while mashing the vegetables, leaving a few lumps and pieces.

Makes 8 servings.

JULIE LOVES HAM, BECAUSE SHE IS ONE, BABY CASSEROLE

Preparing one 4 to 5 pound ham will give you a choice of 100 meals for babies, moms, and dads. Instructions for preparing the basic ham are on the next page.

BABY'S HAM AS JULIE LOVED IT!

⅓ **cup baked ham, cubed**
½ **cup pineapple chunks**

Puree or mince the ham, depending on the baby's development.

Add pineapple chunks to the blender and mix with ham. Then, if more fluid is needed for consistency, add pineapple juice. If pineapple is not accepted or is not available, orange juice will make a nice puree with the ham. Serve and store remainder.

Makes 2–4 servings.

LATER VERSION OF HAM FOR JULIE

¼ cup baked ham, cubed
¼ cup cooked peas
½ cup canned mushroom soup
¼ cup milk
⅓ cup egg noodles, cooked soft

Puree ham, peas, and mushroom soup, adding milk as needed to make appropriate consistency. Either mash the noodles or puree them with the ham mixture. Many babies enjoy chewing finely chopped noodles (pieces about the size of rice grains), starting at around ten to twelve months.

Makes 8 servings.

COLLETTE'S FAVORITE POT ROAST

(The family-sized recipe can be found on the following page.)

¼ cup pot roast beef, cut in ½-inch cubes
¼ cup cooked white potatoes
⅛ cup cooked carrots
1 tablespoon cooked celery (check for strings and
    remove)
1 teaspoon cooked onion (optional)
1 teaspoon cooked green pepper (optional)
⅛ cup cooked peas
2 tablespoons meat gravy
Natural vegetable cooking juices as needed for
    consistency

Puree meat in blender, adding gravy and vegetable cooking juices as needed for consistency. Add vegetables, leaving out the onions and green pepper until the baby is well into "meals" foods. Then blend again, adding more vegetable juices as needed.

Around ten months, or when your baby is ready for a few soft lumps or small pieces of vegetable, continue to puree the meat, but mash or mince the vegetables.

Serve or store in freezer.

Makes 3–4 servings.

COLLETTE'S FAVORITE POT ROAST
(Family Version)

The family ate a pot roast that was between 2½ pounds to
3 pounds of chuck roast prepared as follows:

1 garlic clove
2½ to 3 pounds chuck roast
¼ cup flour
2 tablespoons cooking oil
1 teaspoon instant beef bouillon
1 bay leaf
2 medium-sized white potatoes, cubed
4 large carrots, cut in rounds
1 large green pepper, seeds removed and cut in 1-inch
    pieces
2 or 3 stalks celery, strings removed and cut in 1-inch
    pieces
1 brown onion, peeled and sliced

Finely chop garlic clove. Press garlic into surface of the
roast, then coat all surfaces of the roast with flour.

Heat cooking oil in a dutch oven. Brown the pot roast
on all sides. Drain fat.

Dissolve bouillon in 1 cup hot water, and pour over the
roast.

Add bay leaf, in a tea sieve, to the roast fluid. Lift the
roast so fluid runs underneath.

Cover and bake in an oven at 325 degrees for an hour.
Add all vegetables.

Cook for one more hour and test both meat and vegetables with a fork for tenderness. As the cooking proceeds,
check occasionally to see that sufficient fluids remain in the

dutch oven, add water if required. Baste several times during the cooking process.

Options: Add frozen peas to dutch oven, 15 minutes before the pot roast is served.

Makes 8–10 adult servings.
(See baby version on page 117.)

Tea Sieve information:
Break up bay leaf or other woody seasonings and place them in a tea sieve before adding to cooking foods. This protects the baby from choking on loose pieces.

BABY MEATLOAF

¼ cup Meatloaf*
Vegetable cooking juices as needed for consistency.
¼ cup cooked rice, cooked noodles, or mashed
   potatoes

Puree meatloaf and rice in a blender, adding vegetable cooking juices as needed for consistency.

For meatloaf served with cooked noodles, either blend or mash the noodles with a fork, depending on the baby's development.

For meatloaf served with mashed potatoes, do not mix the meatloaf puree with mashed potatoes. Serve individually. The baby will enjoy having these different flavors separately.

Makes 1–2 servings.

*Follow the recipe on the following page to prepare Basic Meatloaf. Although it may take a bit of effort, it can be frozen to make many baby meals and the adults can enjoy the meatloaf for dinner, in sandwiches, and as a quick-to-fix snack.

BASIC MEATLOAF

2 bunches fresh spinach, or 1 10-ounce package frozen
⅓ pound ground pork
1 pound lean ground beef
1 cup dry bread crumbs
1 pinch nutmeg
1 garlic clove, finely minced
¼ cup parsley, finely chopped (no stems)
½ cup onion, finely chopped
2 large eggs
¼ cup milk
2 tablespoons catsup

Carefully wash spinach by submerging in salted water and agitating. Drain and rinse, running cold water over each leaf.

Remove stems and cook in a covered saucepan with water. Cooking time is about 6 minutes.

Drain spinach, and gently press out any water. Chop, and set aside.

Mix pork and beef together and set aside.

Mix together bread crumbs, nutmeg, garlic, parsley, and onion.

Combine all ingredients with eggs and milk. Mix thoroughly, and press into a loaf pan or a small cake pan.

Brush the top of the meatloaf lightly with catsup.

Bake 1½ hours in preheated oven at 350 degrees. Drain off fat and let cool for about 20 minutes. Slice and serve.

Makes 2 baby and 4 adult servings.

TUNA AND TOAST

2 tablespoons blended tuna mixture (See following
   recipe, Baby Is Taken With Tuna)
2 slices bread

Toast bread and cut in sections (can be either triangles or
toast strips).
   Spread warm tuna mixture over toast, and serve. Older
babies in this age group will probably be ready for finger
foods and will enjoy this tuna mixture.

BABY IS TAKEN WITH TUNA

1 (3¼-ounce) can white tuna (in water)
½ (10¾-ounce) can mushroom soup
¼ cup steamed peas and diced carrots
2 tablespoons steamed celery, finely chopped
Milk as required for consistency

Mix all ingredients except milk together in a saucepan and
heat, stirring in milk as needed for consistency. When mixture is bubbling, remove from heat and serve. At 12
months, blend; mash for more developed babies.

Makes 1 baby and 1 adult serving.

"Chewers" and Adults dinner:
Add ½ teaspoon soy sauce. Heat. Serve mixture in pastry
puff shells. Pastry puff shells may be found in the frozen
food section. Follow baking instructions on the package.
Garnish with parsley and cherry tomatoes.

BABY'S BLEND . . . BROCCOLI AND COD

You can prepare this meal for baby and family at once by increasing the recipe. If the baby cannot chew these finger foods yet, blend the cooked fillets with steamed broccoli, mixed in equal parts. You may use the cooking juices from the broccoli for a thinner consistency as required.

COD FINGER FOODS

½ lb. fresh cod fillets (may be frozen and thawed)
½ cup dry toasted bread crumbs
1 pinch dill seasoning
Corn oil as required

Preheat oven to 400 degrees.
 Rinse fillet and pat dry.
 Cut across the fillet, making 1½ to 2-inch strips.
 Mix the dill seasoning and bread crumbs.
 Brush both sides of the fillets with oil, and roll the strips in bread crumbs.
 Arrange the fillet strips on a nongreased baking pan. Each strip should be separated, not touching.
 Bake in a preheated oven for ten minutes. Fish will flake easily with a fork when done. Ready to serve.

Adults:
When preparing additional cod for adults, double the recipe for two adults, or triple for three. A serving is 8 ounces.

Makes 4 servings.

BABY'S FILLET OF SOLE

2-ounce fillet of sole
1 tablespoon plain yogurt
2 tablespoons bread crumbs

Preheat oven to 400 degrees.
    Rinse fish and pat dry.
    Dip fish in yogurt, covering both sides.
    Place yogurt-covered fish in bread crumbs, coating thoroughly. Set aside baby's portion to be baked with adult's fillets.

Makes 1 serving.

ADULT FILLET OF SOLE

3 4-ounce sole fillets
½ cup plain yogurt
1 cup bread crumbs
3 tablespoons thawed frozen orange juice (undiluted)
1 tablespoon orange peel, finely grated
⅛ teaspoon ground nutmeg

Mix all ingredients in small bowl, except for fish.
    Dip fish fillets in yogurt mixture, and roll in bread crumbs.
    Place baby portion away from adult servings on greased baking sheet or ovenproof dish.
    Bake at 400 degrees from 8–10 minutes until fish flakes easily with a fork.

Makes 1 baby and 2 adult servings.

BABY'S BROILED SALMON

1 salmon steak (1-inch thick)
3 tablespoons butter
1 tablespoon lemon juice
1 tablespoon fresh dill, finely chopped
1 tablespoon dijon mustard

Preparing the Broiler:
Place your broiler rack close to the broiler element. There should be about 4 inches from the top of your baking sheet to the heating element. Preheat the broiler.

Preparing the Baby's Fish for the Broiler:
Rinse the salmon and gently pat it dry. Melt butter in a sauce pan. Add lemon juice and stir. Lightly brush this mixture on the top side of the salmon steak. If you are preparing salmon for the entire family, set the baby's portion aside.

Preparing Adult's Salmon:
Mix lemon/butter with dill and dijon mustard. Brush over top side of the salmon.

To the Broiler:
Gently place the baby's and the adult's portion of salmon on a baking sheet. Use a wide spatula to turn the salmon after 5 minutes. After turning, brush the top side with the butter mixture and return to the broiler for 5 to 10 minutes more. When the fish is done, it will have lost its shiny, translucent appearance, and will flake easily with a fork.

Serving Complements:
For Baby: Pureed asparagus and soft rice mixture
For Adults: Asparagus spears, rice with a sprinkle of soy, and an orange slice.

PASTAS

These quick noodle and pasta creations are for "impatient baby" mealtimes. Use precooked and frozen pasta in 4-ounce individual serving zip-lock bags. (see page 85)

MADELEINE'S MAD ABOUT VEGETABLES

4 ounces precooked pasta, frozen
1 tablespoon butter
2–4 ounces mixed green vegetable puree (see page 104)
1 teaspoon Parmesan cheese

Carefully place precooked pasta in boiling water, for about 1 minute until soft. Drain pasta and cut in ¼-inch pieces. Empty water from pan and dry.

Melt butter in pan. Stirring pasta and vegetable puree into butter, warm for 1–2 minutes.

Sprinkle with grated Parmesan cheese and serve.

Makes 3–4 servings.

CHUCK'S CHEESE AND PASTA

4 ounces precooked pasta, frozen
2 tablespoons poached white fish, mashed or pureed
2 tablespoons steamed broccoli, mashed or pureed
1 tablespoon cheese sauce (see page 130)
1 tablespoon butter

Carefully place frozen pasta in boiling water, for about 1 minute until soft. Drain and cut in ¼-inch pieces.

Heat and stir fish puree, broccoli, and pasta in butter. Top with creamy cheese sauce and serve.

Makes 1 serving.

MACARONI WITH BEEF AND TOMATOES

When selecting ground beef for babies, look for the meat with the lowest fat content.

2 tablespoons ground beef
1 teaspoon green bell pepper, finely chopped or minced
1 tablespoon macaroni (makes 2½ tablespoons when cooked)
2 tablespoons tomato sauce
Sprinkle Parmesan cheese

Mix ground beef with green pepper. Cook in a skillet, stirring so that it will have a crumbled texture. Cook thoroughly; the meat will be pinkish-brown when done.

Cook macaroni according to package instructions and drain.

Add macaroni and tomato sauce to beef and heat.

Many 12–18 month old toddlers will enjoy this meal mashed instead of pureed. Serve with a sprinkle of Parmesan cheese.

Makes 1 serving.

MACARONI WITH CHEESE

1 cup macaroni (makes 2½ cups when cooked)
⅔ cup cheese sauce (see page 130)
¼ cup grated cheddar cheese
½ cup bread crumbs

Cook macaroni according to package instructions and drain.

Mix macaroni with hot cheese sauce.

Spoon mixture into individual serving baking dishes.

Sprinkle cheddar cheese and bread crumbs over the surface, and bake in a 350 degree, preheated oven for 40 minutes.

Makes 6 servings.

QUICK TURKEY AND PASTA DINNER

¼ pound lean ground turkey
1 4-ounce portion spaghetti, precooked (see page 85)
¼ cup canned tomato sauce
Parmesan cheese, to taste

Brown crumbled ground turkey into skillet and cook over
medium heat. Cook and stir until meat is no longer pink.

Gently place precooked pasta in boiling water, using a
slotted spoon. Cook for 1 minute, or until tender, and drain.

Cut pasta in ½-inch pieces and add to skillet.

Next, mix in tomato sauce and stir until heated.

Puree or mash as required for your baby's development.
If you are blending, you may need to add more fluid. Vegetable cooking juices are good. Add a sprinkle of Parmesan
cheese, to taste.

Makes 2–3 servings.

BABY'S TUNA AND NOODLES ENFANT

Egg Noodles:
4 ounces (about 2 cups) egg noodles, precooked
  (according to package instructions)
1 10¾-ounce can condensed cream of mushroom soup
  or equivalent amount of homemade Mushroom
  Marvel soup (see page 133)
Milk as needed for consistency
1 9¼-ounce can white tuna (water pack), drained
1 cup green peas, cooked and drained
1 medium-sized brown onion, finely chopped and
  sautéd
1 teaspoon butter
1 teaspoon soy sauce

Sauté the onion, until translucent; add mushroom sauce and milk to the skillet. Stir, adding remaining ingredients, except the noodles. Heat and stir until bubbling, adding milk as needed for consistency.

Stir egg noodles into the mixture, and reduce heat to simmer for 3 minutes.

If blending is still required for baby, puree in blender. If not, mash with a fork and serve.

Makes 1 baby and 2 adult servings.

SIMPLE SAUCES

Sauces are quick and easy additions to a meal. There are an endless number of variations which spice up foods and create great entree accompaniments.

Learning the basics of making smooth sauces will allow you to avoid packaged mixes or other commercial sauces. Not only will you save money but you will be spared the chemicals and additives often found in the commercial versions.

BASIC WHITE SAUCE

1 tablespoon butter
1 tablespoon flour
¾ cup milk
Salt and pepper, to taste.

Melt butter over low heat in a small skillet. Thoroughly stir in flour. Salt and pepper may be added if baby is allowed these seasonings, otherwise leave them out.

Add the milk and stir continuously. After it bubbles and thickens, cook for one more minute still stirring.

Remove from heat and serve.

Makes 12–1 tablespoon servings.

CHEESE SAUCE

¾ cup basic white sauce
¾ cup grated cheddar cheese or Swiss cheese

After the basic white sauce is cooked, add cheese and stir.
When the cheese is melted, serve.

SAUCY BEEF OR CHICKEN GRAVY

basic white sauce ingredients
1 teaspoon granulated beef or chicken bouillon

Prepare basic white sauce (see page 130), add bouillon to the melted butter and proceed in preparing the sauce.

PARMESAN SAUCE

Basic White Sauce ingredients
¼ cup grated Parmesan cheese

When the basic white sauce has been cooked, mix Parmesan cheese into the sauce and serve.

SAUCE FOR FISH AND VEGETABLES

Basic White Sauce ingredients
½ teaspoon grated lemon peel
Sprinkle chopped chives

When preparing the basic white sauce (see page 130), mix lemon peel with the flour before cooking. Then proceed in preparing the sauce. Serve, topping the sauce with chives.

DILL SAUCE

basic white sauce ingredients
¼ teaspoon dill seed

Mix dill seed with flour when preparing basic white sauce
(see page 130).

SPICY SAUCES

Any of the following seasonings may be stirred into the
melted butter, either separately or together, when making
basic white sauce.

- 1 clove garlic, finely minced
- ¼ teaspoon oregano
- ¼ teaspoon basil
- ¼ teaspoon sage

STRAWBERRY SAUCE

2 cups strawberries, pureed
3 tablespoons sugar
½ teaspoon lemon juice

In blender, blend sugar and lemon juice into strawberry
puree. It's now ready to serve. For a tasty alternative, you
may wish to add a dash of cinnamon.

Leaving sugar out of all foods is not always possible. If

the strawberries are ripe and sweet, they can be served all by themselves.

Makes 4–6 ¼ cup servings.

SOUPS

MUSHROOM MARVEL SOUP

1 cup mushrooms, sliced (fresh)
1 small–medium brown onion, finely chopped
1 cup white potato, cooked and diced (skins removed)
2 cups milk
1 tablespoon butter
Salt and pepper to taste (use in adult portion only)

Sauté mushrooms and onion in a skillet with butter until tender. Season with salt and pepper, removing the baby's portion first if the baby is not allowed this seasoning.

Blend together potato, onion/mushroom mixture, and milk. When you are going to use this as a sauce over vegetables or meats, you will add less milk than when serving soup.

Makes 1 baby and 2 adult servings.

WATERCRESS SOUP FOR BABY AND YOU TOO!

1 bunch watercress
Mushroom Marvel Soup (see page 133)

Remove stems from watercress; place in strainer and wash.

Dip strainer with watercress into boiling water for 30 seconds.

Drain.

Mix blanched watercress with mushroom soup and blend. Remove adult's portion while the pieces of watercress can still be seen. Baby's soup should be thoroughly blended so that the watercress pieces are pureed, and the baby cannot choke or inhale the watercress. Before 18 months it is best to run the soup through a colander and press.

Baby will enjoy this as is. Adults can experience a mini-meal when this soup is served with very fresh French bread.

Makes 2 baby and 2 adult servings.

TODDLERS' TOAST IDEAS FROM ANNABELLE

Bread crumbs:
Wonderful for breading finger-sized pieces of chicken, veal, and fish. Just put pieces of dry toast in the blender and turn it on. Voilà! You have bread crumbs.

Parsley crumbs:

Mix finely chopped parsley with bread crumbs and suddenly the mix becomes topping for a variety of foods. You can even try adding a touch of Parmesan cheese.

Cinnamon toast:

Mix butter, cinnamon, and brown sugar until creamy. Spread on bread, and toast in toaster oven. Remove from oven when mixture bubbles, and is golden brown. Cool, and cut in small squares. Serve when cool.

Cheesy toast:

Spread bread with butter and sprinkle Parmesan cheese over all. Toast in toaster oven. Cut in strips, and serve when cool.

Prune toast:

Mix prune molé (page 146) with butter and spread on warm toast. Cut in small squares and serve.

Milk toast:

Using very dry wheat toast, in a bowl, place 1 teaspoon butter on top. Pour warm milk over all. Serve it immediately. Often children prefer this to cereal.

Pâté toast

Any creamy, pureed meat, chicken, turkey, liver, or ham on tiny squares of toast is delicious and fun finger food.

Egg'n toast

When baby's doctor and baby agree that eggs are fine, it's poached egg time. Poach an egg, mash it with a touch of butter, and spread on top of toast, cut in small pieces.

GELATINS

For warm summer days or just to vary the way your baby sees vegetables; little veggies and fruit floating in gelatin is a sun n' fun solution.

GELATIN GARDEN

1 packet (¼-ounce) unflavored gelatin
½ cup cold water
1½ cups strained or commercial orange juice
½ cup cooked vegetables**
½ cup apples, finely grated

Sprinkle gelatin from packet over ½ cup of cold water and let stand for 1 minute.

Heat and stir gelatin mixture and orange juice over low heat in a sauce pan. Gelatin must dissolve. It will take about 3 minutes.

Pour into single serving dishes, 4 ounces, and chill. When the mixture has not fully set but is like the texture of egg whites (slightly runny but with some firmness), fold in cooked vegetables and grated apples. Let mixture set and serve.

Makes 6 servings

**Suggested vegetable mix:
(Steam in a strainer)
Celery, finely chopped
Carrots, finely grated
Green beans, minced

You may substitute mandarin orange pieces in place of grated apples. This combination is best served to babies able to chew soft fruits.

MIXED FRUIT DESSERT

1 packet (¼-ounce) unflavored gelatin
½ cup cold water
1½ cups unsweetened apple juice
½ cup cooked pear pieces
½ cup ripe bananas, sliced

Sprinkle gelatin from packet over ½ cup of cold water. Let stand for 1 minute.

Mix gelatin water and apple juice in a saucepan. Cook and stir over low heat for 3 minutes. The gelatin must dissolve.

Pour mixture into individual serving dishes and chill.

When mixture has not fully set, but is like the texture of egg whites (slightly runny but with some firmness), fold into fruit mix.

Let mixture set. Serve.

Makes 6 servings.

At some point, your doctor will approve finely ground nuts. Ask about it, the added flavor is very appealing.

For adult dinner salad:
Serve gelatin on red leaf lettuce. Garnish with a spoonful of sour cream or whipped cream. Crushed walnuts may be sprinkled for added flavor and texture.

SUNSHINE ORANGE DESSERT

1 packet (¼-ounce) unflavored gelatin
½ cup cold water
1½ cups orange juice
⅓ cup orange, cut in small pieces
⅓ cup ripe sliced bananas
⅓ cup petite marshmallows

Sprinkle gelatin from packet over ½ cup of cold water and let stand for 1 minute.

Mix, and heat gelatin water and orange juice in a saucepan over low heat, stirring steadily for 3 minutes. Gelatin must dissolve.

Pour mixture into individual (4-ounce) serving dishes and chill.

When mixture has not fully set but is like the texture of egg whites (slightly runny but with some firming), mix orange pieces, sliced bananas, and marshmallows together and fold into the gelatin mixture.

Let mixture set. Serve.

Makes 6 servings.

For adult dessert:
Make a serving cup out of a large leaf of red cabbage on a plate. Place gelatin on cabbage leaf and serve topped with whipped cream and sprinkle of cinnamon.

YOGURT AND FRUIT DESSERTS

When your baby can handle "chunky" foods, you may wish to prepare these recipes with small pieces of fruit rather than blending everything to smooth texture. Each baby is different. Talk with your doctor about your own baby's development in regard to preparation. These light foods will probably remain popular long after babyhood.

STRAWBERRY & BANANA

1 cup plain yogurt
¼ cup ripe strawberries (must be very ripe)
½ ripe banana

Blend and serve.

Makes 4 servings.

RAISED WITH RAISINS AND APPLES

1 cup plain yogurt
½ cup applesauce
¼ cup raisins, stewed (see page 142), and pressed
   through a colander to remove skins

Blend and serve.
   You can add a dash of cinnamon for added flavor when the baby is allowed a few light spices.

Makes 4–5 servings.

RICE PUDDING WITH RAISINS

1 cup vanilla yogurt
½ cup rice, steamed
**¼ cup raisins, stewed (see page 142), and pressed
    through a colander to remove skins**

Blend. Chill and serve.

For adults:
Sprinkle with nutmeg.

                    Makes 5 servings.

MORE YOGURT!

Life has its rainbow! Nature has generously provided us
with gorgeous colors in foods. Babies are fascinated with
colors, and it will be fun seeing how creative you can be
in making foods interesting to them.

1 cup plain yogurt
**¾ cup unsweetened crushed pineapple; drain and
    retain juice**
2 tablespoons red grape juice

Blend pineapple and mix with yogurt and juice. Serve.
    Strain the saved pineapple juice for later use as a bev-
erage or in cooking.

                    Makes 4–6 servings.

VANILLA AND APPLE CRUMB DESSERT

1 cup graham crackers crumbs
4 tablespoons butter
½ cup vanilla yogurt
½ cup applesauce

Melt butter in a skillet and stir in the graham cracker crumbs.

Prepare servings in single-serving dishes, small for baby. Layer the following manner: graham cracker crumbs, yogurt, applesauce, and graham cracker crumbs again.

Party servings can be made more festive by adding whipped cream on top.

Makes 4 servings.

ORANGE CUP DESSERT

1 seedless orange
½ banana
1 cup plain yogurt

Wash orange, and cut in half; scoop out its flesh. Save the peel. Blend orange, banana, and yogurt together. Fill the orange peel with the mixture, and serve.

Party thoughts: These cups are festive for Halloween foods or other parties. Faces can be created with various foods, such as carrots and raisins, or your own artistry.

Makes 2 servings.

RICE IS NICE DESSERTS

RICE N' RAISIN PUDDING

1 cup rice, cooked until soft
⅛ cup raisins, stewed, (see page below), and pressed
 through a colander to remove skins
1 cup condensed milk
Dash cinnamon, (optional)

Blend all ingredients to appropriate texture.
Serve at once or chill. Freeze excess in cubes.

Makes 5 servings.

RICE N' PRUNES

Substitute 4 large pitted and stewed prunes, pressed through
a colander, for raisins in above recipe.

Stewing:
 Raisins—Soak raisins overnight unless otherwise instructed by the package label. Steam raisins for 12 minutes
by placing raisins in a colander over water.
 Prunes—Soak prunes overnight unless otherwise instructed by the package label. Bring water and prunes to a
boil in a saucepan, then simmer for 25 minutes.
 Raisins and prunes will be soft and plump when done.
Save the water so that you don't lose the nutrients.

SWEETS FOR THE SWEETS

GRAHAM CRACKERS AND APPLESAUCE

⅓ cup butter
2 tablespoons sugar
1¼ cups (about 16) graham crackers
2 cups applesauce
½ teaspoon cinnamon

Melt butter in a small saucepan over low heat. Add sugar and stir.

Finely crush graham crackers in a blender, then add crushed graham crackers to melted butter.

Lightly toss the crackers in butter until well mixed.

Press into individual baking dishes (pyrex custard dishes), covering sides and bottom.

Layer applesauce and cracker crumbs, ending with cracker crumbs on top.

Bake at 375 degrees for 4–5 minutes, until top is slightly browned.

Babies will enjoy a little milk with this dessert, or, for the family, top it with a bit of whipped cream and a sprinkle of nutmeg. May be stored in refrigerator overnight, covered. It is also good when served chilled.

Makes 2 baby and 4 adult servings.

PRESENTING PRUNES*

2 prunes
¼ cup unflavored yogurt

Soak prunes overnight (if recommended on package), then simmer them for 30 minutes. Remove pits. They should be plump and tender. Prunes can also be purchased in jars already stewed.

Blend prunes, then press through a cone-shaped colander to remove skin and fiber.

Mix prunes and yogurt. Serve.

When your baby is ready for finger sandwiches, this makes a delightful spread.

Makes 1 serving.

IT'S THE BERRIES

RASPBERRY, BLACKBERRY, AND STRAWBERRY PUREE

Babies love berries. So, here are the steps for preparation: Remove stems and clean. In your food processor or blender, bring to smooth consistency. Pour berries into a colander, and press all of mixture into a bowl, using a wooden spoon.

Throw away the seeds and pulp remaining in the colander. Serve or freeze in cubes.

Adult desserts:
Top angelfood cake with berry puree and whipped cream.

*Note—prunes can bring about loose stools.

or

Make a bed of vanilla wafers in a dessert bowl. Fill bowl with one scoop of vanilla ice cream and top with berry puree.

MADISON'S FAVORITE—LUSCIOUS, RIPE STRAWBERRIES

Madison was sixteen months old yesterday. We shared a bowl of the largest, sweetest strawberries to be found. She was fascinated, completely mesmerized, studying each strawberry as she held it and devoured the red-as-red goddess of fruits.

Pure and simple, as great foods can be, strawberries are perfect all by themselves.

Clean them. Remove the stems. Carefully, serve them one at a time.

MOLÉS
(Pastes for sweeteners and spreads)

Caution: For babies under 2 years, press molé through a colander to remove skins.

RAISIN MOLÉ (PASTE)

1 tablespoon raisins

Soak raisins in a saucepan for 15 minutes. Boil, using the same water, until soft and plump, for an additional 12 minutes. If you prefer to steam, place the raisins in a colander over water and steam for 15 minutes. Blend, adding cooking juices until the mixture becomes a spreadable paste. Press through colander.

Option:
Blend raisin molé using baby formula to replace cooking juices in making the appropriate texture.

Makes spread for 2 pieces of toast.

PRUNE MOLÉ (PASTE)

½ pound dried prunes

Soak dried prunes overnight in water. Cook in a saucepan, using the same water. Bring to a boil, and then simmer for 30 minutes. Remove from heat when plump and soft.

Drain the prunes, saving the juice for a beverage mix or for other cooking requirements.

Using a blender, add cooking juices to make a spreadable paste. Press through a colander and serve.

Option:
Whip 1 tablespoon butter with the yield from recipe. The

entire family will enjoy this as a sandwich spread. Adults will enjoy ground nuts in the mixture.

Makes 10 servings.

Fruits have natural sugars and are preferable to refined sugars as sweeteners. Some combinations may seem strange to parents simply because they aren't accustomed to mixing these foods. Your baby will benefit if you use your creativity in using fruits to sweeten.

These fruits may cause loose stools and should be used in a proper balance with other foods. If your baby is in any way showing signs of a tender tummy, these fruits should be temporarily avoided. On the other hand, if the baby is constipated, this may be an aid in correcting the problem. Consult your pediatrician.

APPLESAUCE TOAST

2 tablespoons applesauce
1 slice toast
Dash cinnamon

Heat applesauce in a sauce pan while you lightly toast bread. Cut the toast into finger-sized pieces, and spoon on warm applesauce. Sprinkle with cinnamon and serve.

Makes 1 serving.

CREAM CHEESE, TOAST, AND FRUIT

2 slices toast
2 tablespoons cream cheese
5 small cantaloupe cubes
5 medium-sized watermelon cubes, seeded
5 strawberries
½ banana, sliced

Cut toast in quarters. Spread cream cheese on quarters of toast. Mix the fruits together. Blend or mash them until the baby can eat soft fresh fruit. That time will likely come during this age period, 12 months–18 months.

Stand the toast around the fruit serving bowl and let the toddler enjoy.

As the baby is able to join the family and share in family food, this will make the entire family happy.

Makes 2 servings.

*5

Fourth Step: Foods For 18–24 Months

If ever a mother needed a "break," this is the time. The best present a dad could give would be three daylight hours when he watches the junior mountain climber. Up on a chair, down squeezing the cat, and in the cupboard taking everything out; this is certainly eighteen months old. The sounds your baby is making may not be real words, but he can copy mom's mannerisms, talk into the phone with gibberish, and bring smiles to any adult's face.

Babies between eighteen months and twenty-four months are active, and have grown to different levels of development. One baby may have molars and start saying real words, while another may not. Some may still prefer pureed baby foods for most of their meals. What your child should eat depends on both development and preference. Generally, though, a child of this age will enjoy holding pieces of food and munching, foods with some texture, foods that stay in the bowl of a spoon until they reach a little mouth.

As your baby grows into the acceptance of foods in this chapter, you can use the recipes, continuing to blend them to the appropriate texture, while gradually decreasing fluids and making coarser textures. Then you will be able to mash the soft vegetables and fruits with a fork, allowing more and more soft lumps, as he develops.

149

At this stage, some babies will chew vigorously during the first part of a meal. As time passes they get tired and the food goes down in solid form. Watch, and take note of what is happening.

You may want to assist with the feeding when the baby tires of self-feeding. You can take a fork and mash the remaining foods. Always be present when your baby is feeding. Supervision, even though from a few feet away, is very important.

By twenty-four months, the baby is drinking from his glass, enjoying finger foods, and proficient enough to start playing with his foods. As long as eating is taking place, along with the play, the meal isn't over.

CEREALS

Making cereal for your baby may also bring better eating to the entire family. The only caution is that when making whole grain cereals for the baby, the grind must be fine. Coarsely ground grains may not be digestible for the young and tender tummy.

Check with your doctor in regard to which cereals are to be introduced. Certainly you will save money and give good nourishment by making your own cereals and blends, or by buying the most basic commercial cereal and adding your own fruits and flavors.

Cereals that are commonly used are listed below. Your pediatrician should be consulted. He or she may add to or subtract from the list.

Oatmeal	Cream of Rice	Cream of Wheat
Barley	Toasted wheat germ	
Millet	Corn meal	

Many fruits look and taste good with cereals. You should still be cautious in serving dried fruits and nuts at this age. Here are some tasty suggestions to serve with hot or cold cereals:

Strawberries • Raspberries • Banana slices • Pureed apricots • Pureed peaches • Raisin molé (see page 146) • Grated apples, cooked in cereal • Grated pears, cooked in cereal • Chopped, canned peaches (syrup rinsed away)

SWEETENERS

Pureed fruits, or—later on—soft, ripe fruits, are much better nutritionally than sugar, honey, or molasses. As the baby begins to join in family meals, it is not expected that sugar, honey, or molasses will never be served; however, you should be aware that the issue is more than nutrition gained from the current meal. By avoiding these sweeteners, the baby is learning what to expect, and to appreciate better eating habits. You are setting standards for a lifetime.

When it comes time to offer some packaged cereals, it is equally important to review labels, limiting sugar and additives. Puffed cereals without anything added are a good choice. History indicates that few babies crawl through toddlerhood without a few fistfuls of Cheerios. Served with milk, or dry, there is a special fascination for the round shape with the hole in the center.

Cheerio! Cheerios are great for baby's first ring. Has there ever been a baby who didn't love to play with these little snacks? "First you have to get it on your finger and then you can eat it."

FRUITS

BAKED APPLES

2 medium sized cooking apples
6 tablespoons brown sugar
½ teaspoon ground cinnamon
Small pinch nutmeg
2 tablespoons butter
Apple juice, or water as needed in baking dish

Wash and core apples, trimming a strip of apple peel from
the top of each apple.

Mix sugar and spices together.

Place apples in a casserole dish for baking.

Pack the sugar and spice mixture into the center (core
area) of each apple.

Place butter on top of sugar, and press down.

Pour apple juice or water, about ½ inch, into the bottom
of the casserole dish.

Bake at 350 degrees for 40–45 minutes, or until tender.
Baste occasionally.

Makes 4 servings.

Serve for breakfast, snacks, or dessert. Baked apples are
wonderful when served slightly warm all by themselves or
with milk, cream, yogurt, or ice cream. Adding whipped
cream, with a sprinkle of nutmeg, to the top makes a great
dessert.

Caution:
In this age bracket, *babies cannot eat the skin of the baked apple.* Remove the skin or scoop out the apple to serve. Pour a bit of the cooking juices on the apple and mash it.

PRISCILLA'S PEARS

2 pears, halved, cored, and peeled
¾ **cup water**
¼ **cup orange juice**
⅓ **cup sugar**
½ **cinnamon stick**
1 teaspoon vanilla

Place all ingredients except the pears in a skillet, and bring to a boil.

Add the pears, turn the heat down to simmer, and cover the skillet.

Simmer for 12–15 minutes, then test for tenderness.

Remove the cinnamon stick and serve.

Serve to your favorite baby either mashed pears, or finger food sized pieces, as he nears his second birthday.

Pears are good either warmed or chilled. They can be the main focus of a salad, eaten alone, or as a dessert with whipped cream and a mint garnish.

Makes 4 servings.

RHUBARB PIE

3 cups rhubarb, sliced
⅔ cup sugar
¼ cup water
2 strips orange peel
1 teaspoon corn starch
1 package (6) precooked individual pie shells

Place sugar, water, and orange peel in a sauce pan, and bring to a boil.

Add rhubarb slices, and reduce heat. Cover, and simmer for about 5 minutes, until rhubarb is tender.

In a cup, mix the corn starch with a bit of the pan juices, and then add it to the pan.

Stir until mixture is thick, and bubbly.

Using a slotted spoon, lift the rhubarb and spoon it into precooked pastry shells. Add a bit of the sauce.

Place a dot of sour cream or whipped cream on top.

Rhubarb has a wonderful flavor, yet many adults have not tried it. Allow your baby to experience foods along with you. Explore new things together.

Makes 2 baby and 5 adult servings.

VEGETABLES

SWEET POTATO FANCY

3 warm, cooked sweet potatoes (about 1 pound)
1 tablespoon margarine or butter
3 tablespoons milk
¼ cup bread crumbs

In a blender, blend sweet potatoes, margarine or butter, and milk to make a thick, creamy texture—it must not be runny.

Use flat, small individual casserole baking dishes (4-ounce size). Fill each casserole with the sweet potatoes and sprinkle with bread crumbs. Place under a broiler for a few minutes to brown the bread crumbs. Test the temperature, and serve warm.

Sweet Potato Fancy is attractive and great to serve for guests. Babies will enjoy being part of the entertaining and the dinner.

Makes 4 servings.

SQUISH–SQUASH

This recipe may not be chewable for toddlers without blending or grinding. Make it for the entire family dinner, leaving the adult's portion whole.

½ pound yellow summer squash
½ pound zucchini
1 pound tiny new potatoes, cooked, (or the equivalent canned)
1 sweet red pepper, medium sized
1 tablespoon olive oil
Salt to taste (may be omitted for baby)
½ teaspoon marjoram

Wash and trim summer squash and zucchini. Cut in bite-sized cubes.

Wash the red pepper, remove seeds, and cut in ½-inch long, very thin strips.

Sauté the red pepper strips in olive oil, for 3 minutes.

Add the squash and potatoes, sauté for 4 more minutes. The zucchini will be a lovely bright green when done.

Using blender, or grinder, prepare all vegetables except potatoes to a granular texture. Potatoes may be mashed.

Make certain that all larger pieces have been removed.

For adults:
Do not blend. Salt and add marjoram. Stir and serve. If your doctor agrees that your baby can have spices, you may wish to season the baby's food with the same seasonings.

Makes 2 baby and 4 adult servings.

CLAUDIA LOVES CAULIFLOWER AND CHEESE

This recipe is for everyone to enjoy. If you want a wee portion for the baby only, *cook less.*

1 small head cauliflower
½ cup mushrooms, sliced
1 tablespoon margarine or butter
½ cup American cheese, grated

Soak cauliflower in salted water, swish it around, and rinse in cold water.

Break cauliflower into flowerets. Steam until crisp, tender. Baby portion must be steamed a bit longer until it is soft.

While the cauliflower is cooking, sauté mushrooms in margarine or butter.

Drain cauliflower, and while still steaming hot, mix with mushrooms and top with cheese. This must be done quickly so that the cheese will melt.

If the cauliflower is not hot enough to melt the cheese, the vegetables can be placed in a baking dish and heated briefly under a broiler until cheese melts. Mash baby's portion with a fork.

Serving suggestions for parents:
This dish is excellent with broiled white fish, a wedge of lemon, and a serving of fresh cooked peas.

Makes 1 baby serving and 4 adult servings.

PARSNIP VEGETABLE CASSEROLE

1½ cups parsnips, peeled and sliced
½ cup carrots, cut in rounds and thinly sliced
2 tablespoons onion, chopped
1 tablespoon butter
Pinch nutmeg
3 tablespoons soft bread crumbs
1 egg, slightly beaten

Boil vegetables in a covered pan for about 18 minutes or until very tender. Drain in a colander.

In a blender, blend vegetables with butter and nutmeg.

Add bread crumbs and egg; blend mix.

Grease a ½-quart casserole dish. Pour mixture into dish.

Bake at 375 degrees for 35–40 minutes. Test doneness by inserting a toothpick into the center of the casserole. It will be done when you remove the toothpick and it is clean.

Serve with mashed soft steamed green beans and chicken textured for your baby's development.

Makes 1 baby and 2 adult servings.

FOUR-WAY MASHED POTATOES

3 medium-sized potatoes
2 tablespoons butter
Milk
Salt lightly to taste

Peel potatoes, rinse, and cut in cubes.

Cook in a covered pan with slightly salted boiling water

for 20 to 25 minutes. Test with a fork to see when potatoes are soft enough to mash. Drain.

Process potatoes with butter in a blender, or mash. Gradually add milk, and blend or mash until potatoes are light and fluffy. Potatoes can be stored, covered in a refrigerator, for 2 days and reheated in a lightly greased skillet, for another baby meal.

Makes 1 baby and three adult servings.

PATTY CAKE, PATTY CAKE MASHED POTATOES

½ cup chilled mashed potatoes
1 tablespoon butter

Form patties. Brown in a buttered skillet over medium heat, about ten minutes, turning once so that both sides are golden brown when done. Serve with meat and a green vegetable.

Makes 2 servings.

PATTIES WITH ONION

1 tablespoon butter
2 tablespoons brown onion, finely chopped
½ cup mashed potatoes, chilled

Sauté onion, drain, and mix with chilled mashed potatoes. Prepare as you would Patty Cake Mashed Potatoes (See above).

Makes 2 servings.

MASHED POTATO PANCAKES

½ cup packaged pancake mix
1 egg
Water or milk (on package instructions)
3 tablespoons mashed potatoes
1 tablespoon cooking oil

Combine pancake mix, egg, and water or milk as instructed on package. Stir, adding mashed potatoes, and additional fluid until the batter will pour from a spoon, as pancake batter.

Heat a lightly greased skillet or griddle, and pour 1 tablespoon of batter for each dollar-sized pancake.

Cook on each side, turning when the surface is bubbly and beginning to dry. The surfaces will be a light brown when done.

Makes 20 dollar-sized pancakes for the baby and family.

BROCCOLI, CARROTS, AND RED PEPPER

6 small broccoli flowerets
1 carrot, sliced in thin rounds
2 red bell pepper strips, very thinly sliced
½ teaspoon butter
1 squeeze lemon juice (optional)

Place broccoli, carrots, and bell pepper in a steamer pan with red pepper strips on top. Steam for 10–12 minutes, using about ½ inch water in the bottom of steamer pan. Test for tenderness with a fork.

Remove vegetables to a serving bowl. Butter lightly, and add a few drops of lemon juice.

Serving suggestions:
Serve this vegetable medley with thin slices of turkey meat and mashed potatoes. Mash or mince the baby's food as needed, removing the bell pepper. The bell pepper flavor will remain. Freeze extra servings.

Makes 6 servings.

MEATS, POULTRY, AND FISH

"Simple foods for tender baby tummies" is still the rule. Meats and poultry can be pureed, minced, or cubed for your baby's appropriate texture and development. Simple foods are still the easiest to make and all that is necessary for your baby. When you want to make something with more flavor for the family, there are food mixtures in these chapters that offer more flavoring and variety.

The transition from very liquefied foods to eating family foods is a gradual process. When the molars match and chewing is possible, your baby may chew for a while and then lose interest or slow down the chewing. That is the time for you to step in and help. Mash the food and help in the feeding. It is good to offer one food that requires chewing and two that do not when planning "early chewing" meals. Eating should always be enjoyable, and not too much work.

MARY'S LITTLE LAMB PATTIES

5 strips bacon
½ onion, finely chopped
1 slice white bread (stale)
2 tablespoons fresh parsley, chopped
¼ cup catsup
½ teaspoon salt (optional)
1 pinch pepper (optional)
¼ cup prunes, stewed and pitted
¾ pound ground lamb

Cook bacon until crisp. Remove excess oil on paper towels, and crumble bacon.

Sauté onion in a skillet using oil from the bacon.

Place the following in a blender: bacon, onion, white bread, parsley, catsup, salt, pepper, and prunes.

Blend on Medium for 30 seconds.

Mix ground lamb with the ingredients from the blender and form into 5 patties.

Broil patties on each side for 6 to 8 minutes. Test to make sure the meat is cooked through.

Serve with a garnish of mint jelly.

Note:
Depending on the baby's development, you can puree, mash with a fork, or cut into finger food sized pieces.

Makes 10 patties.

THANKSGIVING TURKEY DINNER FOR TODDLERS

⅓ cup cooked turkey white meat, minced or cut in
  very fine pieces
⅔ cup mashed potatoes
2–3 tablespoons homemade gravy (see page 131)
Milk as needed for consistency for dressing
1 tablespoon pureed beans
2 tablespoons cranberry sauce, pressed through a
  colander
1 tablespoon turkey dressing

Serve mashed potatoes topped with gravy, pureed green
vegetable, strained cranberry sauce and turkey, slivered or
minced.

Make the dressing easy to eat by blending it with a bit
of milk. Dressing is usually the family tradition that everyone makes the same way, year after year. This is your
baby's first year. Enjoy! The baby will not finish all his
food, but this is Thanksgiving and he should be able to
choose his favorites.

DALLAS COWGIRL'S BURGER LOAF

2 pounds ground beef
1 brown onion, chopped
½ cup black ripe olives, pitted
2 cups tomatoes, diced
1 cup instant oatmeal
¼ cup catsup
1 teaspoon salt (may be decreased)
1 pinch pepper (optional)

Chop black olives.

Cook and stir chopped onions and olives in an oiled skillet over medium heat for 5 minutes. Place in a strainer and very gently press to remove excess oil and juices.

Add the onions, olives, and all other ingredients except the meat to a blender. Blend for 15 seconds on medium.

Thoroughly mix the blended ingredients with meat. Press the meat mixture into a greased loaf pan and bake at 350 degrees for about 1½ hours. Check to see that the ground meat is cooked throughout.

Serving suggestions:
Babies and family will enjoy this loaf when served with chopped steamed spinach and mashed potatoes. Left over loaf makes great sandwiches.

Burger Loaf will serve 6. (Freeze the excess or make a family "Texas Round-up" burger loaf.)

COWBOY'S LIVER PATTIES

1 brown onion, finely chopped
1 tablespoon butter or cooking oil
1 cup ready-to-eat-wheat cereal
2 cups hot water
1 pound cubed beef liver
6 slices bacon, uncooked

Sauté onion in a small skillet with butter or oil.

Stir cereal in with the onion, slightly heating. Remove to a bowl.

Pour hot water into the skillet and add the cubed liver.

Bring to a boil. Reduce heat, and simmer for 15 minutes, stirring occasionally. Drain liver and cool.

Place liver cubes in blender and blend at fairly high speed, adding cooking juices as necessary to keep the blender from overheating. Texture should be granular as appropriate for making patties.

Mix cereal and onion mixture with liver and form into 6 patties. Wrap bacon around each patty, and secure each with a toothpick.

Broil patties for about 4 minutes on each side. The bacon must be crisp when done.

Serving:

Remove toothpick and bacon from toddler's patty, and cut in small, bite-sized pieces.

Cowboy's Liver Patties are enjoyable when served with peas and pasta.

Sometimes babies who have been proficient with the fat round spoon will suddenly decide that using fingers is much better. You can offer the spoon but it is really of no concern. Finger foods are fine!

Serves two little ranch hands, plus a mom and dad.

POACHED FLOUNDER FILLETS

1 pound flounder fillets
½ cup apple juice
1 cup water
1 tablespoon lemon juice
1 tablespoon dill, chopped

Set aside the fillets.

Put remaining ingredients in a large skillet. Bring to a boil. Carefully add the fish fillets, and return to boil. Reduce heat and cover. Simmer for 4–6 minutes. When done, the fish will be flaky.

Serve with tartar sauce.

Makes 2 baby and 3 adult servings.

TARTAR SAUCE

2 tablespoons mayonnaise
1 teaspoon sweet pickle relish, finely chopped
Dash onion salt
Squeeze lemon juice
Pinch parsley, finely chopped

Mix all ingredients. Chill and serve.

Makes 3 servings.

FISH AND GOOD THINGS DINNER

1 canned peach half
1 broccoli floweret, soft steamed
2 ounces pasta rounds, soft cooked
1 piece baked fish fillet (½-inch thick fillet; cut off 2-inch piece)

Cut peach half in small pieces.
    Mash broccoli with a fork.
    Mince fish fillet.
    Mix together broccoli, peach, fish, and pasta.
    This dinner is good for babies who are using a spoon and chewing soft foods.

Makes 1 baby meal and a few shared tastes for mom.

6

Fifth Step: Foods For 24–36 Months

By age two, children are eating portions of adult table foods. No one can tell you exactly what your child is prepared to eat at any specific time. Each child is developing differently. Most children will still need snacks between meals as well as the traditional "three meals a day."

Snacks should not detract from the meal. It doesn't matter what time of day your child gets his nourishment, but it is important that you do not feed sweets close to mealtime. Vegetables will be better accepted when your child is hungry and when sweets have not been offered. Gradually children will fit into the family eating patterns.

It is important that two year olds are allowed to leave the table when they have finished their meal. Adults may linger over a great conversation, but children are full of energy and aren't comfortable being that confined.

Most children prefer each food item to be separated on a plate. Often they will completely finish one food before beginning another.

Small portions on small plates are appealing. Massive amounts of food on a plate overwhelm little people. Pretty little servings encourage the toddler to try all of the food items offered. Never force food if a child doesn't want something. Small servings are the best strategy.

Children often know more than we do about food choices. One baby tried tomatoes and rejected them immediately. Eventually, she ate them and developed red splotches on her skin. Tomatoes simply did not agree with her tender digestive system.

Take the time to sit with your child at mealtime. Happy, loving mealtimes are an investment in bonding. The time will come when your child will want to grab a sandwich and take it with him to go play. On a bright sunny day, he may ask you to come along!

Start good habits by insisting on clean hands before and after the meal. Germs are spread so easily on the hands, and beginning good health habits will carry on when your child goes to nursery school and throughout life.

When your baby wants to hand you something, don't forget to say "thank you." "Please" and "thank you" are the two words that make a world of difference and mealtimes offer an opportunity for using both words many times.

CEREALS FOR FUN AND NUTRITION

OATMEAL ISN'T BORING ANYMORE

If you want to give oatmeal some extra zip, you can check the seasonings and flavors that manufacturers combine with oatmeal in the quick-fix cereal section, or buy old fashioned oatmeal and make your own flavorful variations. Prepare each baby serving when you are going to serve it. Do not store.

Basic Apple Flavor
To get the basic apple flavor, you can follow the package directions on regular oatmeal and substitute apple juice for half of the water required.

Cinnamon Apple Oatmeal
Make Basic Apple Flavor Oatmeal. Just after adding the fluids to the cereal, mix in the following:

Finely grated apple
Soft steamed raisins
Dash of cinnamon

Cook and serve.

Pears and Pecans Oatmeal
Make Basic Apple Flavor Oatmeal. After fluids have been added, mix in small pieces of pear and finely chopped pecan nuts. Check with your doctor to see that your child is ready for nuts. Cook and serve.

Banana and Walnut Oatmeal
Add finely chopped walnuts to the Basic Apple Flavor Oatmeal. Cook and place in serving bowls. Add sliced bananas on top of cereal and serve with milk.

Options:
Vanilla yogurt can be used to top cereal instead of milk.

CREAM OF CORN HOT FRIES

1 cup cornmeal
½ teaspoon salt
3 tablespoons cooking oil

Prepare cornmeal mush according to package instructions (cooking time is about 15 minutes).

Spray a rectangular pan, 7½ × 3½ × 2 inches with nonstick food spray. An ice cube tray without divider is also workable. Pour, and spoon cornmeal mush into the pan.

Cover with plastic wrap. Freeze overnight.

Remove corn meal mush from the freezer dish and place it on a cutting board. Cut in ¼-inch slices.

Fry in greased skillet, turning once until both sides are golden brown and the outsides are crisp.

Serve with pancake syrup. You may cut off the portion you wish to fry and leave the remainder in the freezer for another meal.

Makes 14 toddler servings or 7 adult servings.

SPECIAL CREAM OF RICE

¼ cup Cream of Rice cereal
1 cup water
1 butter patty
Milk as desired

Make regular Cream of Rice using package instructions.

Place in serving bowls. Add one small patty of butter and mix it into the hot cereal to melt. Top with raw brown sugar. Serve with milk.

Option:
Add cinnamon if desired.

Makes 1 toddler or 2 adult servings.

CREAM OF WHEAT CEREAL AND PRUNES

¼ cup Cream of Wheat cereal
1 cup water
1 teaspoon Prune Molé (see page 146)
Milk as desired

Prepare Cream of Wheat cereal according to the package instructions.

Before serving, swirl in Prune Molé, to sweeten according to taste. Top with milk.

Makes 2 toddler or 1 adult servings.

ANOTHER WAY TO MAKE CREAM OF WHEAT OR RICE

Both Cream of Wheat and Cream of Rice can be made using milk as a replacement for water. It makes a nice, rich creamy texture. If you desire, you may add a bit of butter to the hot cereal, mixing it in to melt.

FRUITY YOGURTS FOR BIGGER KIDS

Measure vanilla yogurt and fruit in equal parts.

Any soft fruit that the baby can eat, in small pieces, can be mixed with the yogurt. Cut the fruit in baby-sized pieces and mix the yogurt and fruit by hand.

Suggested Fruits and Seasonings

- Sliced bananas, with a pinch of cinnamon
- Small pieces of ripe peaches, with melba crumbs
- Drained crushed pineapple
- Peeled and seeded mangos, cut in very small pieces
- Blueberries
- Raspberries
- Strawberries
- Cantaloupe, cut in small pieces
- Honeydew, cut in small pieces
- Apples, grated with a small pinch of nutmeg, or cinnamon, and a drop of lemon juice
- Apricot pieces, very ripe and skinned

SUMMERTIME BREAKFAST

½ cup vanilla yogurt
½ cup frozen raspberry puree
1 ripe banana
¼ cup canned, unsweetened crushed pineapple,
   drained

Blend yogurt and raspberry puree.
   Cut banana in rounds, and place on small serving plate.
   Spoon yogurt/raspberry mixture over banana.
Top with pineapple. Serve.

Makes 4 servings.

NO MONKEY BUSINESS
MORNING FRUIT PLATTER FOR
MOMMY, DADDY AND ME

¼ cup fresh ripe strawberries
2 guavas, halved
2 loquats, seeded and cut in halves
¼ cup watermelon balls, seedless
¼ cup honeydew balls

Arrange the fruits on a beautiful plate. Serve and enjoy. A
touch of mint always makes a fruit plate more exciting.

Makes 3 servings.

STILL CANTALOUPE BECAUSE YOU'RE TOO YOUNG

¼ cup ripe cantaloupe, cut in 1-inch cubes
⅓ cup vanilla yogurt
12 green seedless grapes

Place cantaloupe in a bowl and drizzle yogurt on top. Garnish with green grapes. Serve and enjoy.

Makes 3 servings.

BANANA CHEESE TOAST

2 tablespoons low-fat ricotta cheese
½ banana, sliced
2 slices wheat toast

Spread cheese on toast and cover with sliced bananas. Cut in finger-food-sized pieces and serve.

Makes 1–2 servings.

BANANAS AND STRAWBERRIES

4 quartered strawberries
½ sliced banana
8 green seedless grapes, cut in half
2 thin slices kiwi fruit, peeled

Mix together and serve.
   Remember to cover up . . . strawberries will stain clothing.

Makes 2–3 servings.

SNACKS

SANDCASTLE SNACKS

Sandcastle snacks are particularly enjoyed by small fry who are mastering the three major sports: whistling, snapping fingers, and skipping.

APPLES AND PEANUT BUTTER

1 Red Delicious apple
creamy peanut butter as needed for spread

Wash and chill apple. Cut in thin slices, removing the core (remove skin for 2 year olds).
   Spread one side of each slice with creamy peanut butter, and serve.

Makes 2–4 servings.

NONCANDY CANDY

¼ cup dried figs
¼ cup walnuts
1 teaspoon vanilla (alcohol free)
¼ cup shredded coconut
2 tablespoons powdered sugar

Grind dried figs and walnuts; mix together. Flavor with vanilla, to taste. Roll into balls or stick shapes.

Coat with powdered sugar or coconut, alternately.

Options:
Mix 2 tablespoons creamy peanut butter or 2 tablespoons honey into the fig/nut mixture for special flavors.

Makes 14 pieces of noncandy.

CARROT AND CELERY STICKS

1 celery stalk
1 carrot

Wash, trim, and remove strings from celery. Scrape and wash the carrot. Make fine strips, about 2 inches long, from the carrots and celery.

Serve over ice in a bowl. Chilled, they are delicious.

Makes 4 servings.

CELERY AND STUFFING

1 celery stalk
**2 tablespoons pureed meats, cream cheese, or creamy
   peanut butter**
Dash garlic salt

Wash, trim, and remove strings from celery.
Cut crosswise in 1-inch long pieces.
   Stuff pieces with pureed meats and a dash of garlic salt,
or with cream cheese, with or without pimento.
   Another sandbox set favorite is celery stuffed with pea-
nut butter.

Makes about 8 pieces.

TRAIL MIX FOR THE BACKYARD TRAIL

¼ cup Rice Chex
¼ Cheerios
2 tablespoons spanish peanuts
2 tablespoons raisins

Mix together all ingredients, put in small individual bags,
and serve.

Makes 12 bags.

COTTAGE CHEESE AND CRACKERS

1 graham cracker, 2 soda crackers, or 3 wheat thins
1 tablespoon cottage cheese

Spread cottage cheese on crackers and serve.

Beverage suggestion:
Mix carbonated water and orange sherbet.

Makes 1 serving.

TOMATO SOUP ON A FOGGY DAY IN GLENDORA TOWN

1 cup tomatoes, chopped and peeled
⅓ cup milk
Fish shaped crackers

Blend tomato and milk in a blender until it is smooth. Simmer over low heat, until bubbling and heated through. Serve with fish-shaped crackers floating on top.

Makes 2 servings.

ALPHABET SOUP

1 cup chicken broth
¼ cup chopped vegetables
2 tablespoons alphabet pasta
4 crackers

Cook vegetables and alphabet pasta in broth. Cooking time depends on which vegetables you choose (check vegetable cooking chart). Alphabet pasta requires 8 minutes.
Serve with crackers.

Makes 2–3 servings.

STUFFED EGGS

2 boiled eggs (small- or medium-sized)
1 tablespoon mayonnaise
¼ teaspoon prepared mustard
Sprinkle paprika

Cut boiled eggs in half lengthwise, removing yolks. In a small bowl, mix yolks, mayonnaise, and mustard. Stuff the mixture into the egg whites, and sprinkle sparingly with paprika.

Makes 2–4 servings.

FRUITS AND VEGETABLES

Fruits and vegetables are the best snacks possible. Make them pretty by cutting them in fancy shapes. Make flowers, animals, trains, or anything your imagination can design.

SAVE TEETH BY BRUSHING AFTER SNACK
TIME. WHEN A TOOTHBRUSH IS NOT AVAIL-
ABLE, SWISH WATER IN THE MOUTH TO RE-
MOVE PARTICLES BEFORE BACTERIA CAN
DEVELOP.

LITTLE SIPPERS' SIPPERS

Check with the baby's doctor about your baby's acceptance
of raw eggs.

PEANUT BUTTER PARTY DRINK
FAMILY BATCH

*Blend the following at medium speed for 40
seconds:*
2 cups milk
4 tablespoons creamy peanut butter
1 egg yolk
1 cup vanilla ice cream

Whip the following until soft peaks form:
1 egg white
1½ tablespoons sugar
2 drops nonalcoholic vanilla
Small pinch salt

*Add egg white mixture to blender with ice cream
mixture.*
Stir in blender at moderate slow speed, about 1 minute.

Makes 1 toddler and 3 adult servings.

ORANGE AND EGG BREAKFAST DRINK FOR BABY, FAMILY, AND FRIENDS

Blend the following at medium speed in blender:
3 eggs
3 cups orange juice (strained if fresh-squeezed)
¼ cup honey
1 tablespoon lemon juice (strained)

Serve over ice. Garnish with orange slice over rim of glass.

Makes 1 toddler and 3 adult servings.

STRAWBERRY AND BANANA MORNING JOY

Blend the following at medium speed in blender:
1 large banana
½ cup cold water
1 cup cold milk
¼ cup strawberry puree
½ cup vanilla ice cream

Serve, and garnish with a ripe strawberry and sprig of mint.

Makes 3 servings.

YOGURT, STRAWBERRY, AND BANANA

1 small banana
¼ cup mashed strawberries
8 ounces vanilla yogurt

Puree banana and strawberries in blender until smooth consistency.
   Mix puree with vanilla yogurt. Serve.

Makes 2–3 servings.

PINEAPPLE & STRAWBERRY 'FRESHER

Crushed ice
1 cup strawberries, chilled and mashed
2 cups natural pineapple juice

Crush ice in blender and pour into glasses. Set aside.
   Puree strawberries in blender. Add pineapple juice, and blend until smooth.
   Pour mixture over ice.

Makes 3 servings.

GINGER SIPPERS' SNAPPER

Blend in a blender until smooth and fluffy:
6 ginger snap cookies (crumble before adding other ingredients)
1 cup milk
1 cup vanilla ice cream
¼ teaspoon vanilla, nonalcoholic

Serve.

Makes 2–3 servings.

TOOTHY TEETHERS FRUIT CUBES

Freeze fruit juices (not pineapple) in cubes and you will have a wonderful aid for babies with tender gums. These are fun even when the teeth are not popping through.

Using different fruit juices, you will have a rainbow of colors that appeal to little ones.

SALADS

BEET AND CUCUMBER SALAD

1 cucumber, peeled and thinly sliced
1 large or 3 small cooked beets, chilled, and julienned or coarsely grated
Sprinkle garlic salt
Squeeze lemon juice

Place cucumber slices and green onion in a serving dish.

Sprinkle with garlic salt and squeeze lemon juice over the top. Mix.

Serve over chilled beets on individual plates.

This recipe is good for toddlers approaching the third birthday.

Makes 1 toddler and 3 adult servings.

POTATO SALAD WITH BEETS

2 medium-sized potatoes
1 stalk celery, thinly sliced (strings removed)
1 large beet
½ cup mayonnaise
½ teaspoon mustard
¼ green pepper, minced
1 green onion, finely chopped
2 boiled eggs, chilled and chopped
4 lettuce leafs

Boil potatoes in covered pan for 20–25 minutes until tender. Peel, cool, and cube.

Boil beet for 50 minutes in covered pan. Test for tenderness. Peel, and cut into julienne strips. Refrigerate in a separate covered container.

Mix mayonnaise and mustard. Add all ingredients except beets, and lettuce. Chill.

Just prior to serving, drain any juice from beets and stir them gently into the salad.

Serve on a leaf of lettuce.

Makes 1 toddler and 4 adult side dish servings.

CARROT AND RAISIN SALAD

1 squeeze lemon juice
½ large or 1 small apple, chopped in a blender or
   finely grated
1 medium carrot, minced in a blender or finely grated
1 tablespoon raisins, soaked and simmered until soft
2 tablespoons mayonnaise
Milk for creamy dressing consistency
2 lettuce leaves

Mix a few drops of lemon juice into the grated apples to
help them retain their color.

Mix carrot, apple, and raisins together.

In a small bowl, mix mayonnaise with enough milk to
slightly thin it.

Stir mayonnaise into the carrot mixture and serve on a
lettuce leaf.

Excess can be refrigerated for up to two days.

Makes 2–3 servings.

LITTLE PAL POTATO SALAD

1 medium potato
2 hard boiled eggs
1 stalk celery, finely minced
¼ cup mayonnaise
½ teaspoon prepared mustard

Using a small saucepan with a lid, cook potato in boiling, salted water for 25 to 30 minutes, until tender. Drain and peel. Cut in very small cubes.

Finely chop boiled eggs.

Mix potato, egg, and celery together.

Stir mayonnaise and mustard together and add to the potato mixture. Lightly toss and chill.

If you are preparing more for the entire family, you may add chopped green onions and green pepper. Small children will enjoy the simple mixture above.

Makes 1 toddler and 1 adult serving.

PINEAPPLE AND COTTAGE CHEESE SALAD

1 pineapple slice, canned (unsweetened)
2 tablespoons cottage cheese
¼ cup shredded lettuce
1 tablespoon Thousand Island dressing

Cover center of plate with lettuce, and place one pineapple ring on top of it.

Keeping the round shape intact, cut the pineapple rings into bite-sized pieces, then spoon cottage cheese into the center of the pineapple ring.

Top with Thousand Island dressing and serve.

Makes 1 serving.

CHATTER-BOX COLESLAW

¼ cup cabbage, finely minced
1 teaspoon green onion, very finely chopped
1 teaspoon green bell pepper, finely minced
1 tablespoon mayonnaise
2 teaspoons milk
1 squeeze lemon juice
Seasoning salt, to taste
(Finely shredded carrots optional)

Combine and mix cabbage, onion, and bell pepper.
    Make a light dressing combining mayonnaise, milk, and
a few drops of lemon juice.
    Add dressing to the vegetable mixture. Chill and serve.

Makes 1–2 servings.

CHICKEN SALAD

2 tablespoons celery, finely chopped
¼ cup lightly steamed broccoli, chopped
¼ cup cooked white chicken, cubed
¼ cup pasta wheels, cooked and cooled
¼ cup mayonnaise thinned with milk until creamy
Few drops lemon juice

Mix mayonnaise/milk and lemon juice. Set aside.
    Combine all other ingredients, and stir. Add dressing,
and stir again.

Makes 4 servings.

TUNA FISH SALAD

1 3¼-ounce can tuna
1 tablespoon celery, finely minced
1 teaspoon green onion, finely chopped
1 tablespoon mayonnaise, thinned with milk
Few drops of lemon juice
Optional: 4 slices toast

Drain tuna and place in a mixing bowl. Add, and stir lemon juice.

Mix tuna, celery, and green onions.

Add mayonnaise, and stir.

Serve as a salad with toast on the side or on the toast as a sandwich.

Makes 2–4 servings.

QUICK LUNCH SANDWICHES

On a clear day, spread a blanket on the lawn and settle down with your favorite little person for a picnic fantasy. She may find more joy in a little lady bug than her entire toy collection. Nothing can compare with nature.

PEANUT BUTTER AND BANANA SANDWICH

2 tablespoons creamy peanut butter
1 banana, thinly sliced
4 slices raisin bread, toasted

Spread peanut butter on two slices of toast.
   Place banana slices on the surface of the peanut butter.
   Close the sandwiches and cut it into small shapes that the toddler can handle.

Makes 2–4 servings.

CUCUMBER AND MAYONNAISE

2 slices white bread
⅓ small cucumber, thinly sliced
1 tablespoon mayonnaise

Spread a thin layer of mayonnaise on bread.
   Place a single layer of cucumbers on top of mayonnaise.
   Cut the sandwich into magical shapes.

Makes 2–4 servings.

EGG SALAD SANDWICH

1 hard-boiled egg, chopped
1 teaspoon celery, finely minced
1 teaspoon green onions, finely chopped
1 tablespoon mayonnaise
1 dash mustard
2 slices bread

Mix egg, celery, and onion together.
   Add mayonnaise and a touch of mustard. Stir.
   Spread on bread, and cut into finger-sized pieces.

Makes 2–4 servings.

CHEESE AND TOMATO SANDWICH

2 slices wheat bread
1 tablespoon grated cheddar cheese
2 slices tomato, thinly sliced

Toast bread in a broiler on one side.
Turn toast and sprinkle cheese over surface of one piece.
Toast until cheese is bubbling and toast is golden.
Cover cheese with tomato slices.
Close sandwich and cut in quarters.

Makes 2 servings.

PUREED MEAT, POULTRY, OR FISH SANDWICHES

3 tablespoons puree (options listed below)
1 teaspoon mayonnaise or plain yogurt
Dash allspice seasoning
2 slices bread or toast

- lamb
- pork
- beef
- turkey

- ham
- boneless fish or tuna
- chicken

Mix puree with mayonnaise or yogurt; Season with allspice. Spread on bread or toast; close sandwich and cut in four pieces. Serve.

Makes 1–2 sandwiches.

GRAHAM CRACKER SANDWICHES

2 graham crackers
1 tablespoon creamy peanut butter

Spread peanut butter on graham cracker, cover, and enjoy big smiles.

Options: replace peanut butter with cream cheese or cottage cheese.

Makes 1–2 servings.

TUNA SALAD SANDWICH

4 slices wheat bread
1 3¼-ounce can tuna, packed in water and drained
1 stalk celery (strings removed), minced
1 boiled egg, chopped
1 tablespoon mayonnaise
Squeeze lemon juice
Dash allspice seasoning

Set bread aside and mix all other ingredients together.
Spread on bread, cover, and cut in four pieces. Serve.

Makes 2–4 servings.

VEGETABLES

THE ART OF ARTICHOKES

Artichokes are truly special. They have a distinctly different look and taste than most other foods. The leaves of
the artichoke are wonderful finger foods as well as sophis-
ticated fare for the most elegant dinners. The heart of the
artichoke is a delicacy in salads or other foods. Sharing this
food with tots will give them an opportunity to learn about
something wonderful.

Since artichokes are so unusual, they may be viewed
with some skepticism by almost anyone who hasn't savored
their delicate flavor when embellished with a little sauce or
dip. At first trial, the sauce or dip may have more appeal
than the artichoke itself. This may be one of your child's
first ventures into baby gourmet life, so have fun with it.

The first eating experience probably should happen when you are in the mood to lend a helping hand and have some extra time.

Artichokes should be cooked a little more for toddlers than you might cook them for yourself. The meat of the artichoke must be very soft for them to try.

Cleaning and preparing the artichoke:

Plunge the artichoke upside down several times in a bowl of salt water to cleanse. Rinse under cold running water right side up to flush out sand, dirt, or insects.

Remove outer leaves, and cut the base of the stem. With scissors, cut off the top of each leaf, removing the sharp tips.

Place artichokes in a large pan of boiling water. There should be enough water in the pan to cover the artichokes. Add a slight bit of salt. Bring water to a boil again and cover the pan.

Turn the heat down and simmer for at least 25 minutes. Remove the adult's artichokes, and continue simmering for another 10 minutes. The adult's artichokes should be tested to see that the leaves pull off easily before beginning the extra 10 minutes for the baby's serving. Remove and drain upside down.

Artichokes are wonderful served while either warm or chilled. The baby will certainly not eat very much, and the remainder of the super-cooked choke will be great for artichoke hearts in salads, or the leaves may be served chilled along with other appetizers.

Suggested sauces and dips:

Baby's: Mayonnaise or melted butter with a squeeze of lemon.

Adults: Melted butter with lemon, garlic, or dill.

Feeding:
Hold a leaf upside down, placing the fatty meat area over the lower teeth of your toddler. Pull the leaf slowly and the baby's teeth will scrape the soft meat from the artichoke. Yummy!

SAUCES FOR ARTICHOKES AND ASPARAGUS

SOUR CREAM AND DILL SAUCE

Mix the following together and serve in a small bowl:
¼ cup sour cream
¼ teaspoon dijon mustard
1 small pinch dried dillweed

Mix in a small bowl, and cover with plastic wrap.
  Chill for two hours.
  If you wish to increase the recipe for this sauce, it can accompany white fish for another meal.

Makes 8 1-tablespoon servings.

MAYONNAISE AND EGG DRESSING

4 tablespoons mayonnaise
1 hard-boiled egg yolk, finely chopped
1 teaspoon dijon mustard
1 green onion top, finely chopped

Mix in a small bowl and cover with plastic wrap. Chill and serve.

Makes 5 1-tablespoon servings.

TOMATO AND SPICE SAUCE
For Tot and Tot's Friends

This sauce has less spice and seasoning than many adult
recipes. It is still flavorful and the family will enjoy it. If
you wish to add more seasoning, remove the toddlers sauce
first. Having some of this sauce prepared a day in advance
will allow you to serve pasta lunch for the baby or to mix
it with vegetables for more flavor.

1 pinch dried oregano
1 pinch dried parsley
½ bay leaf
1 tablespoon chopped onion
2 tablespoons finely chopped celery
1 small garlic clove, finely minced
1 tablespoon cooking oil
1 8-ounce can tomatoes
2 tablespoons tomato paste

Place oregano, parsley, and crushed bay leaf in a closed tea
sieve.
   Cook onion, celery, and garlic in oil until tender.
   Puree tomatoes.
   Add tomatoes, tomato paste, and tea sieve to onion and
celery mixture.
   Gently boil and stir until the consistency is right, about
15 minutes.
   Remove tea sieve and the sauce is ready to serve.
   Store in the refrigerator.

Makes 4–5 toddler servings.

CABBAGE, CARROTS, AND POTATOES

1 small cabbage
1 medium carrot
1 medium potato

Remove and discard outer leaves from cabbage. Wash and cut a small wedge of cabbage (½-inch wide), for baby's dinner. Store remainder of cabbage for adult dinner.

Peel, wash, and cut carrot in thin round slices.

Peel, wash, and cube potato.

Place potato cubes in a steam basket, and steam for 8 minutes.

Add a wedge of cabbage and the carrot slices to the steam basket; continue steaming with the potato for 12 minutes.

Drain, storing the cooking juices in the refrigerator. Cut in small pieces and serve (potato may be mashed with a fork).

Adults will enjoy cooking juices served over the vegetables. Season with thyme, red chilies, lemon juice and top with finely chopped parsley.

Makes 3 servings.

CRUMBY GREEN BEANS

Squeeze of lemon
1 cup cooked green beans (cut in ½-inch pieces)
2 tablespoons butter, melted
½ cup sour cream
½ cup bread crumbs

Squeeze a bit of lemon over cooked beans.
Spoon 1 tablespoon of butter over the beans, and stir.
Place green beans in individual bake-proof casserole dishes.
Spread sour cream over beans.
Mix bread crumbs with remainder of melted butter.
Scatter crumbs over sour cream.
Bake for 20 minutes at 350 degrees.

Makes 1 toddler and 2 adult servings.

ZUCCHINI IN SAUCE

½ zucchini, medium-sized
1 tablespoon spaghetti sauce (your favorite brand)
Romano cheese

Wash zucchini, and remove the ends. Cut in ¼-inch rounds.
   Steam for about 5 minutes using a small amount of water. Check with a fork for tenderness.
   Drain and stir in spaghetti sauce. Serve and sprinkle with Romano cheese.

Makes 1 serving.

SPINACH WITH A TOUCH OF LEMON

1 pound spinach
1 teaspoon butter
4 lemon wedges

Spinach must be cleaned thoroughly. Remove stems and place spinach in a steamer pan. Steam using ½ inch water, not touching the spinach. Steam for 3–5 minutes (time begins after steam is forming).

Drain.

Mix in the spinach. Squeeze a lemon wedge over each serving.

Try fresh lemon juice on green vegetables instead of salt. Many people prefer the fresh flavor after making this substitution a few times. Taste buds will adjust and the natural vegetable flavors are enhanced.

Makes 2 toddler and 3 adult servings.

VEGETABLE POTPOURRI

3 medium tomatoes, cut in small wedges
1 cup julienned carrots
1 cup string beans, cut in ½-inch pieces (strings &
    tips removed)
1 cup yellow squash, finely diced
1 cup zucchini, finely diced
¼ red bell pepper, cut in 1-inch fine strips
1 quart chicken broth
Garlic and basil to taste (light for toddler)

Place tomatoes and chicken broth in a large pot.

Place mashed garlic and basil in a tea sieve and add to cooking pot.

Bring ingredients in the pot to a boil; reduce heat, and simmer for ten minutes.

Add all remaining vegetables to the pot. Add water as needed for soup. (See serving options, following)

Bring to a boil, reduce heat, and simmer for an additional 10 minutes. Remove the sieve.

Serving options:

Soup

Add alphabet pasta and cook until pasta is done and vegetables are soft. Serve.

Vegetables and pasta

Vegetables may be removed from the broth with a slotted spoon and served over angel hair pasta. Sprinkle with Parmesan cheese.

KABOBS ARE A SHISH TO FIX

Preparing foods together, as a family, can begin early in your toddler's life. Children thoroughly enjoy helping mom choose what foods she will place on the kabob sticks next, and the excitement of watching kabobs cooking over hot coals on a barbecue. It is essential that you supervise children every moment so that they don't move too close to the heat or coals. If you prefer indoor cooking, or when the weather mandates staying indoors, kabobs can be prepared on a broiler.

By placing brilliantly colored foods next to one another on a skewer, yellows, reds, greens, and other colors, the radiant beauty of this meal will sparkle in your children's eyes. Vegetables become more appealing and the flavors mingle to create a nutritious and happy event at mealtime.

Strip the cooked foods, when serving, from the kabob stick and feed the toddler those foods that he can manage and that are appropriate for his development.

Foods to steam slightly before applying to the skewer:

- Green pepper cubes
- Onion pieces
- Zucchini slices
- Carrot rounds

Foods that are not precooked before placing on the skewer:

- Cherry tomatoes
- Pineapple cubes
- Mushroom caps
- Small new potatoes, canned

Foods that are marinated before placing on the skewers:

- Chicken, ½-inch cubes
- Beef, ½-inch cubes
- Halibut steak, 1-inch cubes

Marinate with teriyaki sauce in a sealed bag for 2 hours in a refrigerator before cooking. You may have another preferred marinade. Read bottle instructions regarding quantities.

Assembling the kabob:
Place meats, poultry, or fish alternately with vegetables and fruits on a skewer. Brush with marinade and turn while cooking.

Barbecue Grill:
Cook 10–12 minutes, turning once.

Oven Broiler:
Cook on greased rack, 4 inches below heat for 10–12 minutes, turning once.

VEGETABLES, HAM AND TURKEY BLANKETS

1 slice white turkey meat, cut paper thin
1 slice boiled ham (square shaped in package)
2 tablespoons mayonnaise
1 asparagus spear, steamed very soft and mashed (no strings)

Mix asparagus and mayonnaise.

Spread mayonnaise/asparagus mixture on the ham slice.

Cut it into squares and press pieces of turkey on top.

Serve as finger foods for snacks or lunch.

Makes 1–2 servings.

SPINACH AND CREAMED CORN

1 pound fresh spinach
⅓ cup creamed corn
2 teaspoons butter

Clean spinach, remove stems and steam for 3–5 minutes. Drain.

Heat corn.*

Cut spinach into bite-sized pieces. Mix with corn and a touch of butter. Serve.

The colors are beautiful and the flavors blend like fresh rain in springtime!

Makes 1 toddler serving and 4 adult servings.

*Corn should be pureed if toddler is younger than 30 months.

CABBAGE AND CARROTS

1 medium white potato
1 large carrot
½ cup cabbage, coarsely chopped

Preparation:
Cut potato in cubes and carrot in chunks.

Steam white potato for 8 minutes.

Add cabbage and carrot pieces to the steamer and cook with potato for an additional 12 minutes. Everything should be tender.

Drain and serve on a plate. Mash the potato and carrot with a fork, adding a touch of butter. Cut cabbage in finer pieces if chewing it is a problem.

Note: Steamer broth should be saved for poaching fish. Refrigerate to store it.

Makes 1 toddler and 1 adult meal.

VEGETABLE AND FRUIT SNACKS

At this inquisitive time of life, children are becoming social people. Having friends share in colorful and tasty fresh food snacks is a terrific way to slip into vegetable and fruit nutrition.

Make snack time a party! Use colorful party napkins, straws, and pretty food combinations. A ''happy time'' experience is part of enjoying the food. You can happily guide your children to good health habits.

CRANBERRIES, FRUIT, AND VEGETABLE STRIPS

1 cup sugar
1 cup water
2 cups washed cranberries
½ cup assorted fruit and vegetable pieces
(*suggestion:* peeled apple wedges, fine carrot strips,
banana slices, and your toddler's other favorites.)

Stir and boil sugar and water for 5 minutes.
Add cranberries and return to boil. Reduce the heat and let
simmer for 15 minutes.
   Test to see if mixture is done by dropping a bit of the
juice on a cold surface or plate. When done, it will gel.
   Pour into small individual serving dishes and chill.
   Place the cranberry sauce dish in the center of a serving
plate. Display fruits and vegetables around the sauce. Serve
1 bowl of cranberry sauce with vegetables and fruits.

Makes 6 additional cranberry servings for other meals.

Options For Fruits and Vegetables:

• Chilled carrot and celery strips, (no strings)
• Cooked and chilled asparagus spears
• Round slices of cooked and peeled sweet potatoes
• Wedges of oranges and pears
• Green seedless grapes and banana strips (½ of lengthwise
  cut)

BEANS

In many cultures, beans are a mainstay food item. That may not be so in your home but they are very nutritious, so you may wish to begin including them in your menus. As always, check with your baby's doctor first and try small amounts before full servings.

Between ages two and three years, you will be serving many adult-type meals. Your child may absolutely decline some foods that you are serving. Some of these foods they will grow to like and others may never be accepted. Don't push the issue. Your baby's nutritional needs can be met while feeding foods that he accepts.

PREPARED DRIED BEANS

Wash beans.

Place beans in a pan of cold water and soak them overnight.

Change the water, and cook for approximately 2 hours, or according to package instructions. Changing the water several times during cooking will lessen the gastric discomfort which often accompanies beans.

GARBANZO BEAN SALAD

Garbanzo beans can be purchased, ready-to-eat, in jars at your supermarket. These beans are attractive and flavorful when served on salads.

Place on shredded lettuce all of the ingredients listed.

¼ **head of lettuce, shredded**
¼ **cup diced tomatoes**
1 **green onion top, chopped**
1 **stalk celery, very finely diced**
1 **carrot, shredded**
¼ **cup garbanzo beans**

Salad dressing, Italian or vinaigrette (as preferred)

Makes 1 toddler and 4 adult small salads.

PANSY'S RAVE NOTICE BEAN SOUP

Pansy's soup is a complete "nippy" weather, by-the-fire-place meal for the entire family. Make it on a rainy day when you would like a wonderful and rich aroma wafting throughout your kitchen.

Measure ¼ cup each of the following and wash them all together:

- Lentil
- Black beans
- Kidney beans
- Navy beans

Wash beans in a big pot with 6 cups of water; bring them to a boil. Turn the heat off and soak them overnight.

In the morning, change the water, bring to a boil, and begin cooking over low heat. Stir occasionally. Check the water level, adding water as needed.

You might want to change the water several times (see page 206).

Sauté the following together, except for tomato sauce, until cooked, but not soft:

2 large carrots, diced
1 brown onion, diced
4 stalks celery, diced
2 whole garlic cloves, finely chopped
1 cup tomato sauce
Pinch oregano
Salt and pepper to taste

Mix sautéed vegetables and tomato sauce in with beans and continue to cook. Stir occasionally and check water level.

Cook until ready to serve for dinner. Sourdough bread is a great accompaniment.

Makes 1 toddler serving and 4 adult servings.

BAKED BEANS AND HAM DINNER

½ cup oven baked beans, canned
¼ cup precooked ham, minced
1 teaspoon teriyaki sauce
8 pineapple cubes, canned

Heat baked beans in a saucepan.

Brown, and heat precooked ham. As the ham begins to brown, drizzle a thin layer of teriyaki sauce over the ham and turn. Heat for one more minute.

Mix ham with beans and serve. Place pineapple cubes on the side.

Makes 3 servings.

GARBANZO BEANS IN A WHIMSY SALAD

This recipe is good for toddlers approaching their third birthday.

¾ cup garbanzo beans
8 cherry tomatoes, halved
1 cucumber, cubed
1 cup lettuce, shredded
1 avocado, sliced
1 teaspoon lemon juice
1 dash celery salt

Mix garbanzo beans, cherry tomatoes, and cucumber together.

Make a bed of shredded lettuce on serving plates, placing bean mixture on top and ½ of avocado slices around the edge.

Puree ½ avocado, lemon juice, and celery salt. Spoon onto salad and serve. Adult portions will be enhanced with a drop or two of tabasco.

Makes 1 toddler and 4 adult servings.

THE INTERNATIONAL GARBANZO BEAN OPEN SANDWICH

Drain **1 15-ounce can garbanzo beans** and place in blender.

Add the following to blender:

1 tablespoon lemon juice
3–4 drops sesame oil
1 teaspoon olive oil
2 tablespoons chopped parsley
Dash paprika
¼ clove garlic, pressed
2 tablespoons red pimento, drained
1 tablespoon creamy peanut butter

Blend, and serve on quartered slices of whole wheat bread or pumpernickel.

Serving suggestions:
Serve on small plate with cubes of Swiss cheese, ripe olive slices, and tomato wedges.

Makes 1 toddler and 5 adult servings.

PUREED COOKED DRIED BEANS

Wash and cook beans according to instructions on page 206. Use a food processor, blender, or hand mill to make a puree. Use cooking juice from tomatoes or water to reach the appropriate consistency. Children will not like it too tacky. Ask your toddler's doctor when it is time for the following foods. Each child is unique and beans can bring about different responses in the digestive system.

TACOS WITH BEANS

1 corn tortilla
1 tablespoon bean puree
2 teaspoons cheddar cheese, grated
¼ small sized tomatoes, diced
1 tablespoon shredded lettuce
1 tablespoon cooking oil

Heat bean puree.

Cook tortillas in an oiled skillet, turning once, when air pockets develop in tortilla. Do not overcook or the tortilla will be too crisp for your toddler. Blot between two paper towels, and remove to rack, folding in half.

Spread bean puree inside of tortillas.

Sprinkle grated cheddar cheese on top of hot beans. Fill with diced tomatoes and shredded lettuce. For toddlers, cut into smaller pieces.

Makes 1–2 servings.

OVEN-PREPARED TORTILLAS
AND BEANS

4 flour tortillas
2 tablespoons brown onions, finely diced
1 tablespoon cooking oil
⅓ pound ground beef
¼ cup bean puree, warm
¼ cup cheddar cheese, grated
⅓ cup tomatoes, diced
½ cup lettuce, shredded

Wrap flour tortillas in foil and place in a 350 degree oven for about 10 minutes.

Sauté onions in an oiled skillet.

Add ground beef and cook, stirring so that meat is crumbled. Drain cooking oil.

Spread warm bean puree on each tortilla. Add ground meat with onion.

Top with grated cheddar cheese.

Add tomato and lettuce. Roll tortillas so that the mixture is enclosed in the tortillas.

Cut in 2-inch lengths for the toddler.

Adults will enjoy sour cream, ripe olives, and salsa as additions to these happy tummy happenings. Guacamole is another south-of-the-border enticement.

Makes 4 tacos. (Toddler may not finish one, but he will try because they are so delicious.)

MEAT, POULTRY, FISH, AND EGGS

LITTLE GOBBLERS' MEATBALLS

3 tablespoons ground turkey meat
1½ tablespoons soft cooked rice
1 tablespoon apricot puree
2 tablespoons bread crumbs

Mix ground turkey and cooked rice thoroughly. Form into miniballs.

Roll miniballs in apricot puree, then in bread crumbs.

Cook in lightly greased skillet, turning until all sides are brown. It is done when the turkey is no longer pink.

Makes 1 serving.

TURKEY AND RICE SCRAMBLE

1 teaspoon cooking oil
2 tablespoons ground turkey meat
2 tablespoons soft cooked rice
2 tablespoons peach puree

Lightly oil and heat small skillet. Add turkey meat and rice. Stir until hot. Turkey meat will no longer be pink when done. Add peach puree and mix.

Cool a bit, and serve.

Makes 2 servings.

TURKEY MEETS PASTA IN A SKILLET

1 teaspoon cooking oil
2 tablespoons ground turkey meat
1 4-ounce serving of precooked spaghetti
Sprinkle Parmesan cheese

Lightly oil and heat a small skillet. Add turkey meat and cook, stirring until done when the meat is no longer pink.

Chop precooked spaghetti into grain-sized pieces and mix in with turkey while continuing to stir. Over low heat stir and add Parmesan cheese. Serve when pasta is warmed through.

This makes a convenient 2 toddler servings. It is difficult to predict when your child will be particularly hungry and it is easier to be prepared.

Makes 2 servings.

PATTY'S GROUND TURKEY PATTIES IN SAUCE

1 pound lean ground turkey
¼ cup carrots, finely grated
¼ cup green pepper, minced
Sprinkle paprika
1 cup chicken broth or homemade broth
1 cup small bow tie pasta
1 10¾-ounce can mushroom soup

Mix turkey, carrots, and green pepper, and form into small patties.

Lightly sprinkle paprika on top side of patties.

Brown both sides of patties over medium heat in a lightly oiled skillet.

Add chicken broth and pasta to the skillet. Bring to a boil, then cover and simmer on low heat for 15 minutes.

Stir in mushroom soup and continue stirring until sauce bubbles.

Serve with green steamed vegetable.

Makes 1 toddler and 2 adult servings.

TURKEY BURGERS

Young children like buns with burgers, and they really appreciate having buns that are small. Soft dinner rolls are excellent for child-sized buns. For little hands, they are much easier to handle than the standard burger bun.

Form turkey burgers from lean ground turkey. If the buns

are square in shape, form the turkey patties to match. Patties for the young should be thin for tiny mouths.

Cook turkey patties in a skillet, turning once. Cook until the outsides are golden brown and the insides are no longer pink. Be certain that the meat is cooked throughout. Place patties on buns.

Serve with mayonnaise and a small amount of mustard.

GROUND BEEF MINIBALLS IN SAUCE

¼ pound lean ground beef
2 tablespoons mashed potatoes
Cooking oil for frying
4 tablespoons mushroom soup (canned or fresh)
2 tablespoons milk

Mix ground beef and mashed potatoes. Form into mini-meatballs.

Cook in a lightly oiled skillet, turning to brown on all sides until it is no longer pink. Drain oil.

Add mushroom soup and milk to the skillet, stir, and heat. Serve.

Makes 2 servings.

FISH STICKS

1 3-inch cut white fish fillet
2 tablespoons natural yogurt
Cooking oil, ¼-inch in skillet
2 tablespoons bread crumbs

Cut fish fillet into finger-food-sized pieces.

Roll fish in natural yogurt, then in bread crumbs.

Cook in oiled skillet, turning once until done. Both sides will be golden brown. Allow 3–4 minutes on each side for ½-inch fillets, and 5–6 minutes on each side for 1-inch. Fish will flake easily with a fork when done.

It takes minutes. Cooking time depends on thickness.

Makes 1 serving.

TUNA ENTREE FOR ONE

(Maybe there is enough for Mom to have a bite too!)

1 teaspoon butter or oil
1 tablespoon onion, finely chopped
1 tablespoon green pepper, finely chopped
3 tablespoons rice cereal flakes
1 3¼-ounce can tuna
1 egg, slightly beaten

Sauté onions and green pepper in butter or oil. After cooking, place onions and green pepper in strainer to drain.

Mix rice cereal, onions, peppers, and tuna in a bowl.

Add beaten egg; mix and form tuna patties. Brown in an oiled skillet turning once, and cook until done.

Makes 1–2 servings.

VEGETABLE FISH STEW

1 medium white potato, cubed
1 brown onion, sliced
1 large carrot, cut in bite-sized pieces
1 white fish fillet
1 teaspoon soy sauce
¼ teaspoon ginger, grated and peeled

Preparation:
Steam white potato for 8 minutes.

Add onion and carrot to the steamer pan. Continue steaming for 12 minutes.

Drain vegetables, saving juices in the steamer pan.

Rinse white fish fillet and pat dry. Cut the fish into several fairly large pieces (checking for bones).

Place the fish in the (hot) steamer pan cooking juices, adding more water if necessary. Add soy sauce and ginger to the cooking water. Simmer with a lid on the pan for 10 to 15 more minutes.

Serve the fish, vegetables, and some of the juices in a flat soup bowl.

Makes 1 toddler and 1 adult serving.

MISS MUFFET'S CHICKEN MYSTIQUE & ENGLISH MUFFINS

¼ cup Swiss cheese, shredded
2 slices brown onion, pulled apart in rings
1 teaspoon butter
½ can condensed chicken soup
¼ cup plain yogurt
1 cup cooked turkey, cubed or slivered
2 English muffins, split
12 spears of very small and tender asparagus
   (steamed, and then chilled)
paprika

Spread grated cheese on English muffin halves. Place in broiler close to heating element. Remove when cheese is bubbly.

Sauté onion with butter or oil in a saucepan. Add chicken soup, yogurt, and turkey. Stir and heat.

Place English muffin halves on individual plates.

Cut asparagus spears to lengths that will fit English muffins, and place them on top of cheese.

Spoon chicken sauce with turkey on top of asparagus, and sprinkle paprika lightly on each. Serve, cutting toddler's serving into small pieces.

Makes 4 servings.

QUICK CHICKEN HAPPY MEAL FOR THE WHOLE FAMILY

4 English muffin halves
1 can mushroom soup
¼ cup milk
½ cup peas, cooked
1 cup cooked chicken meat, cubed or shredded
1 dash soy sauce

Toast English muffin halves in broiler.

Mix mushroom soup, peas, chicken, and a dash of soy sauce in a skillet. Stir in milk to thin. Heat and serve over English muffin halves. Serve toddler ½ serving; he may ask for more!

Makes 4 servings.

CHICKEN DRUMMETTES

When little drummettes are approved by your baby's pediatrician, you will see pure joy on your little angel's face.

8 chicken wings
½ cup honey sauce (recipe follows)

Rinse chicken wings and pat them dry. Cut the wings in two parts. Discard the wing tips.

Pushing the skin up slightly on the drummette, make miniature drumsticks. Place them in a single layer in a baking pan. Brush the tops with sauce. Bake at 375 degrees 20 minutes.

Turn the drummette, and brush with sauce again. Bake for an additional 15 minutes, or until chicken is tender.

Serving: These are messy. Eating of this recipe absolutely requires mom's supervision. Toddlers will handle them with less mess if you scrape off a bit of the sauce. Mom will love it, sauce and all. Toddlers will work on one drummette for a long time!

Makes 4 servings.

HONEY SAUCE

6 tablespoons catsup
1 tablespoon honey
1 tablespoon vinegar
1 pinch garlic salt

Stir all ingredients together and brush on chicken before cooking.

ST. PATRICK'S DAY BLARNEY AND CORNED BEEF DINNER

¼ cup Mom's and Dad's corned beef and cabbage
1 scoop boiled potatoes (mash for toddler)
½ teaspoon butter

Mince the cabbage and corned beef in your blender. Prepare the cabbage separately first. Remove it from the blender and, without rinsing the blender, add the corned beef and mince. Serve each on a plate with buttered mashed potatoes.

Makes 1 toddler meal.

DON'T FORGET TO WEAR AN ADORABLE GREEN HAT AND LOOK VERY HARD FOR THE FOUR LEAF CLOVER

SPECIAL TREAT GREEN CLOVER LEAVES

1 package green Jell-O

Prepare green clover leaves several hours in advance. Using package instructions, prepare green Jell-O and pour it on a rectangular dish in a thin sheet. Chill and set. Using a "clover leaf" cookie cutter, press out the leaves and lift them to plates with a spatula.

PASTRY SHELL BEEF PIE

6 frozen pastry shells, baked and cooled (use package
   instructions)
½ cup canned new potatoes, sliced and drained
¼ cup chopped onion
1 10¾-ounce can condensed cream of mushroom soup
Milk as required for consistency
1 cup cooked beef, cubed
¾ cup cooked diced carrots and peas
Pinch thyme
Dash soy sauce

Place onion and new potatoes in a buttered skillet, and
brown until onion is tender and potatoes begin to brown.

Add mushroom soup and milk, sufficient to make a
creamy consistency. Then add beef cubes, peas, and carrots.
Season with thyme and soy sauce. Heat and stir until bubbly.

Place each pastry shell on a serving plate and fill with
beef mixture. Serve.

Options: Lamb, chicken, or tuna can be substituted for beef.

Makes 6 servings.

A GLEAM IN YOUR EYE ON THE 4TH OF JULY

Memories are made in the evening air with bonfires wafting their smoky fragrances and stars twinkling into sight.
The food tastes better than ever before and after all the
tummies are full and the sparklers have given their last

sparkle, a toddler can cuddle up in a mother's lap and rock to sleep under a sleepy moon.

JULY 4TH DINNER À LA BARBECUE

8 little dinner rolls
¼ pound ground pork
¾ pound ground beef
Season All, to taste
1 brown onion, sliced
Mustard to taste

Mix the pork and the beef. Form into patties and barbecue.

Sprinkle with seasoning and turn once, making certain that the meat is cooked through. Serve on dinner rolls (just the right size for a toddler).

For toddlers, spread a small amount of mustard on the buns.

For adults, more mustard and add slices of onion.

Serve with Little Pal Potato Salad (see page 186). Lemonade is great with this and is healthier than carbonated beverages.

Makes 8 little burgers (adults will eat 2, toddlers 1).

SLIVERS OF LIVERS

1 teaspoon butter
1 teaspoon brown onion, finely diced
1 chicken liver, cut in half
1 slice wheat toast

When you cook a whole chicken, save the liver for a wonderful and nourishing baby entree. Rinse the liver under cold water and pat dry.

Place butter in a small skillet. Sauté liver with diced onion. Cook until the liver is barely pink and the onions are soft and tender. It will take about 5 minutes.

The liver mixture is good when pureed and served on toast.

Option: Add diced liver and onion to an egg and scramble.

Makes 1–2 servings.

DINNER OMELET PANCAKES

1 egg
1 tablespoon milk
1 tablespoon chopped, steamed vegetables, cheese, or meat

Options: onions, mushrooms, broccoli, green beans, green bell peppers, hard cheeses, cottage cheese, slivers of ham, bacon bits, chicken, or turkey. (Use your imagination.)

Lightly beat the egg with a small amount of milk. Add vegetables, cheese, or meat, and stir.

Pour into a heated, oiled skillet. Tilt the skillet so that the egg mixture covers the entire skillet bottom. Cook and turn as a pancake, about 1 minute on each side. Egg will be glossy and moist, but done throughout.

Babies enjoy a sprinkle of powdered sugar on top. Cut into finger-sized pieces.

Makes 1 serving.

EASTER BUNNY HAM DINNER

2 tablespoons ham puree
1 pineapple ring
2 tablespoons Little Pal Potato Salad (see page 186)
2 tablespoons soft cooked green beans, minced
Marshmallows for as large a bunny as you choose
Crispy rice cereal (about ¼ cup for 4 marshmallows)

Heated marshmallows can be molded into shapes. Make the shape of a bunny's body and cover the outside surface with crispy rice cereal. The whiskers, ears, eyes, and nose can be made with cake frosting, raisins, carrot strips, and maraschino cherries—or whatever else you want to use to create the bunny.

Spoon heated ham puree into the center of the pineapple ring. Serve with potato salad, and green beans, and a marshmallow bunny.

PANSY'S EGG SHELL DECORATIONS FOR EASTER

Start this project one week before Easter

Save your egg shells when you cook with eggs. Fill the half shells almost to the top with potting soil. Sprinkle a few seeds of winter rye seed on top. Cover with a bit more soil and water.

In about 4 days the seeds will sprout and, voilà, there will be a miniature garden lawn. Sprinkle tiny jelly beans on and around the egg shells on the table. The little 1-inch chicks from your local drug store along with the eggs and green grass will make a wonderful centerpiece for the Easter dinner.

Use caution that two year olds don't choke on jelly beans. At this age they are for decoration only.

WONTONS, PIZZA, AND WOK FOOD

MAMA, I WONTON KISS

Keeping little baby fingers busy is great fun. Making wonton foods can be a "mommy and me" event. Much of the preparation is accomplished without using anything hot or sharp. In short, it is a safe way to begin cooking together.

Wonton skins are little flour wrappers, rolled into very thin squares. Packages contain about forty skins and can be found in the chilled-deli section of most supermarkets.

- Mom makes the filling for the wonton skins.
- Mom and little one can place the filling on the wontons.
- Mom and her assistant can stick the wonton edges together.
- Now mom takes over for the cooking!

WONTONS AND FILLING

8 wonton skins
2 tablespoons pureed meat, chicken, turkey, liver, or fish
1 teaspoon mayonnaise
1 dash mustard
1 teaspoon green onions, minced
1 dash garlic salt
1 sprinkle Parmesan cheese

Preparation and cooking may be accomplished in different ways. Read on to see the many ways you can prepare and enjoy wontons.

Fillings for wonton skins can be a mixture made with pureed meats, chicken, turkey, liver, or fish. Purees can be combined with a bit of mayonnaise, or a touch of mustard.

For flavor, you can add a sprinkle of finely snipped onion greens, a dash of garlic salt, Parmesan cheese, or pureed vegetables. Make your own flavor selection; be cautious about foods or textures that might cause choking. The mixture should be pasty when spooned onto the wonton skin.

Putting Wontons Together:
Place wonton skins on a flat surface. In the middle of the squares, center one rounded teaspoonful of filling.

Dip your finger in a bowl full of water and run the moistened finger around the edges of the wonton.

Pull one corner of the wonton catty-cornered, forming a triangle. Press all the edges together.

Again, moisten the corners and twist them slightly while pressing them together.

Note: Moisture on edges and points must be sufficient to allow edges to firmly stick together when pressed.

Cooking the wontons:
Boil 6 cups of water in a large pot. Using a slotted spoon, carefully place wontons, one at a time, in the boiling water.

Turn the heat down and gently simmer the wontons for 5 minutes.

One at a time, remove the wontons, using the slotted spoon so that they will drain. Hold each one under cold water to rinse and place them on a tray, separated from one another.

How to serve wontons:
Prepare vegetable soup by cooking vegetables in stock saved from boiling chicken. Make up your own recipe or use carrot rounds, ½-inch pieces of string beans, thin sliced onion, small squares of green pepper, and/or other vegetables of your preference.

Place wontons in the bottom of flat-style soup bowls and carefully pour and spoon the vegetable soup into the bowls.

For a toddler who is beginning to eat soft foods and chew them satisfactorily without choking or gagging, this is a good food. Until he is big enough, smash the vegetables with a fork and cut the wontons into bite-sized pieces. Prepared so that the foods are all soft, it won't be long before a toddler can eat this as the family does.

PETITE PIZZA

1 package (6) refrigerator biscuits
2 tablespoons spaghetti sauce
1 tablespoon grated cheddar cheese

Roll biscuits until they are very thin, about ⅛-inch.

Place rolled biscuits on baking tray, separated from each other. Spread a thin layer of spaghetti sauce over each biscuit. Sprinkle cheddar cheese on top of sauce.

Bake at 350 degrees for 10–12 minutes, until biscuits have risen and cheese is bubbly.

Makes 6 pizzas.

VEGETABLE & TURKEY PIZZA

1 package (6) refrigerator biscuits
2 tablespoons ground turkey, cooked
1 teaspoon red bell peppers, finely chopped
2 tablespoons broccoli, chopped and cooked
2 tablespoons spaghetti sauce
3 teaspoons grated cheddar cheese

Roll each biscuit very thin (about ⅛-inch thick)

Place each biscuit on a baking sheet, not touching.

Sprinkle cheddar cheese on top.

Bake at 350 degrees for 10–12 minutes. Cheese will be melted and edges golden brown.

Top pizza with remaining ingredients, beginning with spaghetti sauce.

Makes 6 pizzas.

LET'S TAKE A WOK TOGETHER
OR
STIR UP A PARTY WITH STIR-FRY FOODS

When children approach the stage of having friends over for meals, sitting at a low table on the floor with cushions will set the stage for a party mood.

Chopsticks can be purchased at the super market. Whenever you think that the children are old enough to use chopsticks without endangering themselves, they will be fun to try. In other countries everyone in the family uses chopsticks. We advise careful supervision so that games don't develop that result in "poking" and "playing."

Once you start "wok parties" they will be a part of your continuing menu plan. So we add this bit for the future. Approaching age five, fortune cookies are great fun to try. They are also available in the supermarket.

If you want to have a fortune cookie message that spells out beginning reading words, often you can remove the message with tweezers and replace it with your own special message.

The Wok

Stir-fry can be cooked in a skillet or in a wok. One of the reasons that woks are so effective is that after the vegetables have been cooked, they can be pushed away from direct heat by making a hole in the center of the vegetables. This is possible because the sides of a wok slope upwards away from the center of heat. Often you will use this "hole" to make sauces that cook best when not mixed with the vegetables.

If you use a skillet, you can make the sauce in a sauce pan and then add it to the vegetables.

GINGER VEGETABLES

1 cup carrots, sliced in thin rounds
1 cup small broccoli flowerets
¼ cup celery, thin sliced (width cut)
¼ cup canned sliced water chestnuts
4 tops green onions (cut to 1-inch lengths)
1 tablespoon cooking oil
½ teaspoon peeled and grated ginger root
Stir-Fry sauce (recipe follows)

Pour 1 tablespoon of cooking oil into wok (add more if needed).

Add carrots and stir-fry for 1 minute.

Add remaining vegetables and water chestnuts, sprinkling ginger over all.

Stir-fry for 4 minutes until crisp but tender.

Push vegetables out from the center of wok and up the sides.

Add sauce to the center of the wok.

Stir the sauce rapidly. The sauce will thicken and bubble.

Continue stirring for one more minute over heat. Stir the vegetables into the sauce and serve.

This recipe is only acceptable when the toddler is close to the third year.

Serves ½ cup to toddler with 3 adult servings remaining.

STIR-FRY SAUCE

1 teaspoon corn starch
⅓ cup pineapple juice
1 teaspoon soy sauce
1 teaspoon brown sugar

Stir all ingredients together and cook in center of wok until it begins to thicken.

MIXED VEGETABLE STIR-FRY

½ cup peas
½ cup small-sized broccoli flowerets
½ cup shredded carrots
½ cup green beans, cut in 1-inch lengths on the bias
2 tablespoons cooking oil
5 large mushroom caps
¼ cup fresh sprouts

Steam vegetables, leaving out mushrooms and sprouts. Cook until they are crisp-tender (see steam cooking chart, page 104) and drain.

Slice and sauté mushrooms in wok.

Increase heat and add vegetables to the wok, except sprouts.

Stir and cook for about 4 minutes. Add sprouts to the wok and stir for an additional 2 minutes. Add sauce, prepared as below in sauce pan. Stir and serve.

Makes 1 toddler and 3 adult servings.

Sauce:
¼ **cup juice from steaming vegetables**
1 teaspoon brown sugar
1 teaspoon soy sauce
¼ **teaspoon chicken bouillon**
1 teaspoon cornstarch

Mix all ingredients together. Make a hole in the middle of
the wok vegetables when they are done. Push the vegetables up the sides of the wok. Pour the sauce ingredients
into center of wok, stir, and cook until it bubbles and begins
to thicken. Then, mix the sauce in with the vegetables for
one more minute, stir, and serve.

Serving suggestions:

• Serve over chow mein noodles
• Serve rice on the side, topped with stir-fry sauce and a
  dash of soy sauce
• Garnish with fresh orange slices and a sprig of mint on
  top

CHICKEN IN A WOK

1 chicken breast, cooked, skinned, and cubed
1 tablespoon cooking oil
½ cup carrots, sliced in paper-thin rounds
½ green bell pepper, cut in ½-inch squares
¼ cup fresh bean sprouts
4 green onion tops, cut in 1-inch lengths
½ cup pineapple chunks
4 tablespoons teriyaki marinade
2 packages Ramen noodles

Prepare Ramen noodles according to package instructions and drain.

Heat cooking oil in a wok. Add carrots and stir-fry for 2 minutes.

Add remaining vegetables to the wok and continue stir-frying for 3 minutes, adding more oil if necessary.

Add pineapple, chicken cubes, and teriyaki marinade. Stir-fry for two more minutes and serve over Ramen noodles. Grind chicken, mash vegetables, and cut ramen in short pieces until toddler can chew without changing the texture.

Serving suggestions:
Place a plate of mixed fresh fruits in the center of the serving table. Green grapes, orange slices, and tomato wedges make attractive and tasty additions.

Makes 1 toddler and 3 adult servings.

MOMMY AND ME—QUICK
SHRIMP & VEGGIES

You can make a delicious and exotic lunch for two in minutes. Good for toddlers who are almost 3 years.

⅛ cup cabbage, finely chopped
⅛ cup carrots, in thinly sliced rounds
4 small broccoli flowerets
1 green onion, finely chopped
⅛ green bell pepper, cut in small squares
6 cooked shrimp, medium-sized
1 tablespoon cooking oil
1 teaspoon soy sauce
1 teaspoon catsup
½ teaspoon mustard

Heat a tablespoon of oil in a wok or skillet. Add carrots and stir-cook for 2 minutes. Add the additional vegetables and continue stirring and cooking until the vegetables are crisp-tender, approximately 5 minutes.

Add the shelled shrimp to the wok or skillet and stir for about 3 more minutes until the shrimp are heated through.

Add mixture of soy sauce, catsup, and mustard. Stir briefly over heat and serve.

Makes 1 toddler and 1 adult serving.

FRUITS AND DESSERTS

SNACKER CRACKER DESSERT

14 graham crackers
¼ cup melted butter
Whipped cream if desired for topping

One of the following fruits and flavorings:

- Applesauce with a dash of cinnamon
- Peaches, chopped into chunks
- Equal parts of banana slices and papaya
- Equal parts of sliced strawberries and bananas

Mix graham cracker crumbs and melted butter in a skillet. Stir and brown.

Press crumbs around the insides of a custard dish and fill in layers of fruit and crumbs. Make the top layer crumbs. Top with whipped cream.

Give A Fig For Dessert

Really ripe figs are so sweet and flavorful all by themselves that we suggest, "Why fix what works?" So, serve them just as they are!

The deep red skinned varieties are especially enjoyable. Peel them and break them up a bit.

Figs are apt to make toddlers have looser stools, so beware of serving more than one at a time.

Guavas

Green-skinned guavas are great! Cut in half, scoop out the fruit within . . . and enjoy!

FROZEN PASTRY SHELL DESSERTS

Children will enjoy individual servings. Frozen pastry shells can be used for many different desserts, for parties, or just to make mealtime fun.

Frozen pastry shells can be purchased in most supermarkets. You can bake them in advance and cool them, putting the dessert filling in at serving time.

Filling Choices:

- Sliced fresh peaches topped with whipped cream
- Raspberries topped with sour cream, sprinkled with cinnamon and brown sugar
- Strawberries and whipped cream
- Bananas and whipped cream
- Lemon pie custard filling
- Vanilla pudding mixed with blueberries
- Chocolate pudding
- Cooked sliced apples seasoned with cinnamon, nutmeg, and sugar
- 1 scoop of vanilla ice cream topped with any fruit puree
- Two vanilla wafer cookies placed upright in ice cream

TRICK AND TREATS HALLOWEEN FUN!

Who said jack-o-lanterns have to be pumpkins? Navel oranges, nice, big, and orange are great for making faces and are just the right size for a toddler to play with. When the fun is over, peel it and enjoy the sweet flavor.

Clear plastic wrap and little satin bows will turn everyday fruits into fabulous trick-or-treat favors. Buy a few pounds of seedless green grapes. Break them into stems with about ten grapes each. Wrap them in plastic wrap and tie with an orange bow or black bow. You can do the same with raisins, wheat thins, licorice, and popcorn. Healthy foods can be made appealing, and make the event fun while saving the tummy aches.

TAPIOCA PUDDINGS

One box of tapioca pudding mix will make many servings for your toddler or family members. Read on for some special flavor combinations and colorful surprises.

TAPIOCA, STRAWBERRIES, AND HONEYDEW

1 box tapioca pudding mix
¼ cup ripe strawberries
½ cup honeydew melon balls

Prepare tapioca pudding mix using instructions on package. Chill.

Puree strawberries in a blender.

Swirl strawberry puree through the tapioca pudding. Avoid overstirring.

Prepare small honeydew melon balls and place them around the bottom and sides of a pretty glass serving bowl.

Fill the dish with pudding and serve.

Makes 6 servings.

TAPIOCA, STRAWBERRIES, AND BANANAS

Prepare as for above recipe, but substitute sliced bananas for honeydew melon balls.

TAPIOCA PUDDING AND PEACHES

Prepare as above recipe, substituting small pieces of peach for other fruits and lining the serving bowl with peach slices.

Serving suggestions:
Top with a bit of sour cream, a sprinkle of brown sugar, and a dash of cinnamon.

FRUIT IN A BOAT

1 pineapple
¼ cantaloupe, cubed
¼ cup green seedless grapes
½ cup watermelon, cubed

Snip the leaves of the pineapple leaving 2 inches on the end.

Cut the pineapple in half lengthwise. Leaving the shell intact, remove the pineapple.

Core the pineapple and cut the fruit into small pieces.

Mix all fruits together and serve them in the shell of the pineapple.

Serving suggestions:
Sprinkle toasted, shredded coconut on top. Serve with miniature sweet rolls.

Makes 1 toddler and 4 adult servings.

SUNDAE, MONDAY, ALL WEEK LONG

Nonstick food spray
8 graham crackers, crumbled
1 cup miniature marshmallows
4 scoops chocolate ice cream
4 tablespoons chocolate syrup

Spray nonstick food spray on small baking sheet, or pie tin.

Cover pan with graham cracker crumbs and place marshmallows on top. Melt marshmallows under broiler. It takes only a minute or two, so watch carefully and remove when the marshmallows turn golden brown.

Spray nonstick food spray on two large serving spoons and use both spoons to scoop graham cracker/marshmallow mixture.

Scoop ice cream in a sundae dish and cover with cracker mix. Pour chocolate syrup on top and serve.

If it's a party, add whipped cream and a maraschino cherry.

Makes 4 servings.

FRUIT KABOBS

Fruit is for the entire family meal. Many tots in this age group will get their fruit in a bowl without a skewer. Your child will grow into an appropriate age group (6 years old) for skewers and will be thrilled the first time they get a kabob like Mom and Dad. In the meantime, prepare the kabob for your toddler and mom can strip the fruit off of it when it is time to eat. Parents and older children can use the skewer, and children adore eating foods that adults are eating.

Preparation:
Using wooden skewers, alternate fruits that are in season. To give you the idea, here are some options: small cubes of cantaloupe; green seedless grapes; pineapple chunks; whole, medium-sized strawberries; honeydew cubes, and more. Make your color pattern and place fruits one by one on a skewer.

Snip the sharp tips off of the skewers after the fruit has been secured to avoid children sticking themselves. We place a red grape over its end.

Serving Suggestions:
1 scoop of lime ice garnished with mint, 2 kabobs, and a few vanilla wafers.

7

Travel, Travel, Travel

WHAT'S A MOTHER TO DO?

Traveling with a baby can be a joy or your worst nightmare. Keeping foods and water as much like the cuisines at home, and having them available at the first baby squeal, will help you and the baby have a good time.

The travel foods listed here are not separated by age groups. Take only those foods that are appropriate to his stage of development, as shown throughout.

FOODS THAT DON'T REQUIRE REFRIGERATION OR COOLING

- Bananas
- Ripe, soft fruits (prewashed)
- Unopened jars of baby food
- Premixed, canned baby formula
- Baby cookies
- Baby crackers
- Small packages of baby cereal
- Boxed juices (Aseptic drinks)

- Bottled baby water
- Finger sandwiches
- Thin carrot sticks

CONVENIENT FOODS THAT REQUIRE REFRIGERATION OR THERMAL CONTAINERS

- Yogurt
- Cottage cheese
- Puddings
- Home made vegetable and fruit purees
- Home made meat, fish, and poultry purees
- Jell-O mixtures

These foods must not be served if the chilled temperature has not been maintained. They are suggested for short travel schedules. After warming, unused foods must be thrown out.

MORE ABOUT TRAVEL

Travel often makes for conflict in a baby's normal schedule. Planning for either short- or long-term travel requires taking along all the necessities for the baby's care and also providing extra comfort items so that the baby's normal schedule is maintained as much as possible.

Many modes of travel, from road to air, require a baby to be restrained in a car seat. When babies go to sleep, they often lean their heads to the side in an unnatural position. There are inflatable neck cushions that will give the baby a place to rest his head comfortably. Deflated, they take up very little space.

When a baby is potty training or has been trained, it is often difficult to find an appropriate restroom. Experience on trains, cars, and airplanes has reinforced the hassle that this causes. Every mother is concerned about germs, easy access, and all the discomforts attending ''bathrooming.'' Once again, the inflatable object comes to the rescue. There is an inflatable baby potty. You place a disposable plastic bag in the cavity and over the edges. After pottying has taken place, remove the bag, and deflate the potty for easy storage.

Your car should be equipped with a shade, which will minimize overheating and sun exposure. The temperature inside your car changes quickly. NEVER LEAVE A CHILD UNATTENDED WHEN YOU LEAVE YOUR CAR. Even when you think that you will be gone for just a few minutes, it is dangerous. Should you be distracted momentarily or be delayed, your child could be killed. Each year, children are lost in this manner.

Disposable diapers are not to be forgotten. Even those babies who are in the transitional stage of being between diapers and potty should not be counted on to remember when the excitement of new sounds and sights takes over.

Umbrella strollers are lightweight, easy to pack, and will relieve a lot of back stress. To enjoy travel, you need to have as many conveniences as possible without overburdening yourself with the weight and bulk of your packing.

The best advice possible is to not rely on supplies that anyone promises to have ready for you. Airlines mean well and so do many others, but people get busy and no one cares about your baby as you do.

Aseptic drink boxes of water are wonderful to pack because they are small and square. These can be very helpful when you need clean water for clean-up jobs and faces. Wipes are great when water is not handy.

Traveling, visiting, and the out-of-doors are great socializing opportunities. By planning ahead and bringing food mills, spoons, bibs and such, you can have a great time together.

EATING AT RESTAURANTS

When you are dining out, there are many foods in restaurants that can be easily mashed, or ground in a hand-churned food mill.

- Mashed potatoes
- Cooked pears or peaches
- Applesauce
- Crackers
- White chicken meat
- White fish
- Fresh soft-cooked vegetables
- Jell-O
- Puddings
- Cottage cheese
- Mixed vegetables from soup

Thermal bags, bottle holders, and travel items will help in keeping baby foods hot or cold. Special attention must be given to keeping foods at safe storage temperatures.

Take a plastic mat or a cover with you to restaurants. Often baby trays are wiped with dirty cloths before being given to your baby. Babies are apt to remove their foods from the serving dishes and eat them off of the trays. Clean is better.

Small trips to the ice cream parlor or trips around the world require two most important items: baby wipes for cleaning faces, hands, bottoms, and mothers, and disposable trash bags. What did we ever do without them?

LAST BUT NOT LEAST

Find a place where gentle breezes blow wafts of flower petal fragrance. Cushion your sweet baby with the softest green grass. Look up and listen for the muted *whoosh* of birds' wings. Soar, glide, and be free. Let a crystal beam of sunshine dance on your baby's hair. Share a red, red strawberry and a loving hug.

These are the golden presents of a lifetime; food of the soul.